ORTHODOX LENT, HOLY WEEK AND EASTER

Orthodox Lent, Holy Week and Easter

Liturgical Texts with Commentary

by
HUGH WYBREW

ST VLADIMIR'S SEMINARY PRESS
CRESTWOOD, NY 10707-1699
1997

Library of Congress Cataloging-in-Publication Data

Wybrew, Hugh
    Orthodox Lent, Holy Week, and Easter: liturgical texts with commentary/by
Hugh Wybrew.
       p.   cm.
    Originally published: London, England: S.P.C.K., 1995.
    Includes bibliographical references.
    ISBN 0-88141-162-0 (alk. paper)
    1. Orthodox Eastern Church. Triodion. 2. Orthodox Eastern Church.
Pentekostarion. 3. Orthodox Eastern Church—Liturgy—Texts. I. Title
    BX375.T75W83   1997
    264'.019—dc21   97-5317
                                           CIP

First published 1995 by S.P.C.K., London, England

ISBN 0-88141-162-0

PRINTED IN THE UNITED STATES OF AMERICA

TABLE OF CONTENTS

Preface to the American Edition

This book was originally published in the United Kingdom. It has been written by an English Anglican (Episcopalian) for Christians of Western tradition in Britain. That is why the Introduction begins with a brief description of Lent, Holy Week and Easter in the Western tradition. The basic pattern of this central season of the Christian year in the Western churches is similar to that in the Orthodox Church. But the two traditions sometimes differ in the themes that run through their services. My intent in writing the book was twofold: first, to help western Christians understand something of the biblical and theological content of Orthodox services during the Great Fast and Passion Week, culminating in the Feast of Feasts at Easter; and second, to provide them with liturgical material which might enrich their own meditation on human sinfulness and God's saving work in Christ's suffering, death and resurrection.

The book is rooted in my own experience of Orthodox worship. I first took part in the services of Lent, Holy Week and Easter when I was a student a the Russian Orthodox Theological Institute of St Sergius in Paris. Later I had the good fortune to be able to be there again for Holy Week and Easter. Subsequently I have taken part in these services in the Orthodox church in Oxford, and in Romania, where I was the Anglican chaplain at the Church of the Resurrection in Bucharest for two years. More recently, during my three years as Dean of the Anglican Cathedral of St George in Jerusalem, I was able for three years to attend Holy Week and Easter Services in the Russian, Romanian and Greek Orthodox churches in Jerusalem. The experience of the appearance of the New Fire from the Holy Sepulchre on Holy Saturday in the Church of the Resurrection is unique for any Christian.

My earlier book, *The Orthodox Liturgy,* has proved to be of use for Orthodox as well as western Christians. It seems that this book too has been found helpful by English-speaking Orthodox Christians in Britain and North America. There are of course English translations of Orthodox liturgical texts, both in Britain and in North America, which are widely used liturgically. But they are not always easily accessible to lay people, whether Orthodox or non-Orthodox, and relatively few people possess copies of them. This book is not designed for liturgical use. It contains only a small selection of texts. The introduction to each section, and commentary on it, are meant to help ordinary Christians to become more aware of the meaning of Lent, Holy Week and Easter, and to participate more profoundly in the prayer of the Orthodox Church as it celebrates the suffering, death and resurrection of Jesus Christ.

I am grateful to St Vladimir's Seminary Press for publishing it in North America, and so making it available to a wider circle of Christians of all traditions. I hope it will contribute to the growing understanding of Orthodoxy among non-Orthodox, and help all who read it to enter more fully into the liturgical life of Orthodoxy. In so doing it may make a contribution to the movement for reconciliation among the different Christian traditions, as well as helping us all to become more faithful disciples of the crucified and risen Christ.

Hugh Wybrew
St Mary Magdalen, Oxford
January 1997

Introduction

In all those Western churches whose pattern of yearly worship is shaped by the traditional calendar, Lent, Holy Week and Easter follow the same basic lines. Easter, the celebration of the resurrection of Jesus, is the central festival of the Christian year. Many churches celebrate the Paschal Vigil, with its strong baptismal note, as at least in theory the main celebration of the Christian Passover; though it is often held on the evening of Holy Saturday. That day has in practice no well-defined theme for most Western Christians, in spite of its being one of the days of the "Triduum Sacrum," the three holy days of the death, burial and resurrection of Christ.

The rest of the Holy Week preceding Easter has three days whose themes are clear: Passion or Palm Sunday, with its commemoration of the Lord's entry into Jerusalem, and the solemn singing or reading of the passion; Maundy Thursday, celebrating the Last Supper and institution of the Eucharist, often with the washing of feet; and Good Friday, the solemn proclamation of the suffering and death of Jesus. The Monday, Tuesday and Wednesday of Holy Week also have their themes, less prominent because within the overarching context of the passion. In the Roman rite they are Jesus' anointing in Bethany on Monday, Judas' betrayal of Jesus on Tuesday and Wednesday: themes embodied in gospel readings which "Lent, Holy Week and Easter" provides also for the Church of England. A recent tendency in Western churches has been to emphasize the special character of Holy Week, distinct from the rest of Lent.

Lent itself begins on Ash Wednesday, with its call to repentance and use of ashes as a sign of penitence, and the themes of the

1

Sundays in Lent include the temptation of Jesus on the first Sunday, his transfiguration, and, in the Roman rite, the raising of Lazarus. The passion and death of Jesus, and the need for his followers to take up the cross themselves, become stronger as Lent progresses towards Holy Week. There is the occasional hint of resurrection beyond death. The preliminary Sundays which formed part of both Roman and Anglican rites, the so-called "gesima" Sundays, have disappeared in all the reformed calendars, as an unnecessary preparation for a preparation. The 1980 Alternative Service Book of the Church of England provides three Sundays before Lent, but their themes are not related to Lent itself.

These liturgical themes, expressed in Scripture readings, hymns and prayers, provide the basic material for Christian reflection and meditation during these central weeks of the Christian year. Supplemented by the daily readings at the Eucharist, and by those of Morning and Evening Prayer, they constitute a wholesome spiritual diet for those who try each year to enter into the liturgical prayer of the Church and make it their own. Used year after year, they help to form in us "the mind of Christ," the Christ who gave himself willingly to suffer and die, in order to reconcile the human race and all creation to the Father.

The Byzantine Orthodox tradition shares in all essentials the same basic pattern in its preparation for, and celebration of, Holy Week and Easter. But in detail the pattern contains its own distinctive features. There are still preliminary Sundays in the Orthodox calendar, each with a theme quite different from those of the old Western "gesima" Sundays. Lent begins on a Monday, with Vespers of Monday the previous Sunday evening, which ends with a ceremony of mutual forgiveness. The Sunday themes are distinct, too, with a mid-Lent Sunday devoted to the veneration of the cross. The Saturday before Palm Sunday is a commemoration of the raising of Lazarus; and the Saturday of Holy Week is a definite commemoration of the burial of Christ, and his descent into the place of the dead.

Orthodox liturgical texts for Lent and Holy Week abound in biblical imagery and allusion, and are rich too in doctrinal content. They leave no room for doubt that the one who suffered on the cross is none other than the Son of God, or God the Son, the Second Person of the Trinity. "God was in Christ reconciling the world to himself." That phrase, from 2 Corinthians 5:19, sums up the Christian understanding of the suffering and death of Jesus; and the Orthodox texts never cease to marvel, often in striking language, at the paradox of the God who cannot suffer, becoming one of his own creatures in order to share their pain and mortality, so that he can heal them and raise them to share his own undying life. Underlying their understanding of redemption is their Christian faith in the incarnation.

Liturgical traditions of other churches are not only of intellectual interest to Christians: they can often make an important contribution to our own devotion, and help us to enter more fully into the mystery of God's suffering and saving love. This book gives a small selection from the liturgical texts used by the Orthodox Church during Lent, Holy Week and Easter. They are intended to do two things: first, to give Western Christians some idea of the way in which Orthodox Christians try year by year to appropriate the Paschal mystery, the saving events of Christ's suffering, death and resurrection; and second, to provide material which can be used chiefly in personal prayer, but perhaps also in public worship, to enlarge and enrich our observance of this central celebration of the liturgical year. A selection of the hymns, for example, could be used, in an Anglican context, after Morning or Evening Prayer instead of the usual prayers "after the Third Collect." Over a good many years I have found these texts of great value both personally and in public worship, and can only hope that they may be of help to others.

3

The Orthodox texts for the pre-Lent Sundays and for Lent and Holy Week are found in the Lenten Triodion, one of the several liturgical books of the Orthodox Church. The version most easily available in the United Kingdom is that of *The Lenten Triodion,* translated by Mother Mary and Bishop Kallistos Ware, published by Faber. It is not a complete translation, but gives the texts of the Sundays before and during Lent, the first week in Lent, some other significant days, and Holy Week. It does not include the texts of the Easter services, which are found in the Pentecostarion. It uses as far as possible the traditional liturgical English of the 1611 Authorized (King James) Version of the Bible and the Book of Common Prayer of 1662 of the Church of England. It was felt that a translation in a more contemporary idiom would be more suited to the purpose of this book, intended primarily for personal use. The translation of the texts selected has been made from the Greek, and I am very grateful to Francis Warner, Lord White Fellow in English Literature at St Peter's College, Oxford, for his help and encouragement in making it. Orthodox hymnography refers frequently to the Scriptures, containing many biblical phrases or allusions. For these I have used the New Revised Standard Version. English Anglicans may find the occasional echo of the 1980 Alternative Service Book.

Chapters 1 and 2 provide as background a brief sketch of the development of Lent, Holy Week and Easter in the Byzantine tradition, and of their pattern now in the Orthodox Church. Each section of the book begins with a brief liturgical introduction, and ends with a short theological commentary.

1

The Development of Lent, Holy Week and Easter in the Byzantine Rite

The Origin of Easter

At the heart of the Christian faith is the conviction of Jesus' disciples that God had raised from the dead the one they had seen die on the cross. Jesus died at the time of the Jewish Passover; and it is reasonable to assume that when the earliest, Jewish, Christian communities celebrated Passover, they did so with the death and resurrection of Jesus in mind. Paul, writing to the Corinthian Christians, says that "our paschal lamb, Christ, has been sacrificed. Therefore let us celebrate the festival, not with the old yeast, the yeast of malice and evil, but with the unleavened bread of sincerity and truth" (1 Cor 5: 7). Whether or not that points to the existence of Easter as a definite annual festival, it is reasonable to suppose that from a very early time, if not from the very beginning, the Christian Passover was at the heart of the life of the Church of the new covenant, as the Jewish Passover was at the heart of the Church of the old. It celebrated the exodus effected by Jesus' death and resurrection, the passage from death to life, from the slavery of sin to the freedom of God's children.

The Early Christian Passover

The Christian Passover was certainly celebrated by the second century. It was a single, unitary celebration of both the death and the resurrection of Jesus, and was also a celebration of the salvation brought about by those events, into which believers can enter here and now. In most churches it was celebrated on the Sunday after the Jewish Passover, on the ground that it was on a Sunday,

5

the first day of the week, that Christ rose from the dead. In others, however, particularly in Asia, it was celebrated on the same day as the Jewish Passover, the 14th of the month Nisan, whichever day of the week that might be. The Quartodecimans, as they were called by their opponents, continued to maintain their own observance, which they held went back to the Apostle John, into the fifth century. The Council of Nicea, in 325, decided in favor of the Sunday observance. In the majority of churches the Christian Passover was celebrated at a service beginning on Saturday evening, and lasting until the early hours of Sunday morning. It was widely believed that Christ's coming again would take place during this Paschal Vigil, to complete God's work of salvation.

This one-day celebration was preceded by a one-day fast, held on a Saturday among those who kept Passover on a Sunday. Since by the second century Fridays and Wednesdays had become established as regular fasting days, it was in practice a two-day fast that led up to the Christian Passover. By the middle of the third century a fast lasting six days had come to be observed in many places, so providing the background to the development of a full Holy Week observance in the following century. But the unitary celebration of death and resurrection was still maintained; and by the third century the rites of Christian initiation had come to be associated with the Paschal Vigil. For some weeks those who had asked to be admitted to full membership of the Christian community had been preparing for the sacraments of initiation by fasting, exorcism and instruction. During the Scripture readings which made up the first part of the Vigil these catechumens were baptized and confirmed, and then joined the rest of the congregation for the celebration of the Eucharist towards dawn. It was the climax both of the Vigil and their own initiation.

Holy Week in the Fourth Century

It was only towards the end of the fourth century that the six days immediately before Easter developed into Holy Week as we know it. The provision of a sequence of liturgical observances for the week seems to have been made first in Jerusalem, in the episcopate of Cyril, bishop of the holy city from about 349 to 386. During the fourth century the standing of Jerusalem was transformed. In 326 the Empress Helena, mother of the Emperor Constantine, paid a visit to Palestine. While she was there the supposed site of the crucifixion and a rock-cut tomb believed to be that of Jesus were discovered. The Emperor commanded a magnificent church, known as the Martyrium, to be built on the site, previously occupied by a temple of Venus. Close by, the tomb of Christ was marked out, and soon covered by a great rotunda, called the Anastasis, the Church of the Resurrection. Other sites linked with the last week of Jesus' life were also established; and by the time Cyril became bishop there were two more churches, on the Mount of Olives: the Eleona, built over the cave where Jesus had given his final teaching before his death, and the Imbomon, commemorating his ascension. Another church had been built on Mount Zion, associated with the Last Supper and Pentecost. Gethsemane, too, was provided with a church commemorating the agony in the garden. Jerusalem had become an important focus of pilgrimage, and the home of communities of ascetics.

It was perhaps in part to cater to the many pilgrims who came to keep the Christian Passover in Jerusalem that Cyril devised the liturgical observances of Holy Week, which rapidly became a model for churches elsewhere. We are fortunate in having a full description of them written by Egeria, a Spanish nun who spent three years in the Middle East from 384 to 387. She was in Jerusalem for Lent, Holy Week and Easter in 384. A close observer of liturgical practice, Egeria wrote for her sisters back home; and it was no doubt descriptions such as hers which encouraged the spread of Jerusalem observances elsewhere.

The special services of the Great Week, as it was called in Jerusalem, began in effect on the Saturday before Palm Sunday. A vigil was held from Friday evening to Saturday morning in the church on Mount Zion, ending with the Eucharist. On Saturday afternoon the congregation gathered in Bethany at the church built over the tomb in which tradition held Lazarus to have been buried. There the raising of Lazarus, brother of Mary and Martha, was commemorated. The next day, the beginning of the Great Week, was the commemoration of Christ's entry into Jerusalem. In the afternoon, services were held in the churches on the Mount of Olives, after which a procession made its way down into the Hedron Valley, and so up into the city, the people carrying branches of palm.

On the Monday, Tuesday and Wednesday of Great Week there was an additional service each day. Monday's was held in the Martyrium, and the gospel told of the mother of the sons of Zebedee's request to Jesus for places of honor for James and John in his kingdom. On Tuesday it was held in the church in the Eleona, and commemorated Christ's last, apocalyptic discourse to the disciples. On Wednesday night a special visit was paid to the Anastasis after the extra service, where the gospel was read commemorating Jesus' anointing in Bethany in the house of Simon the Leper and Judas' agreement with the priests to betray Jesus.

On Thursday in Great Week the usual services were held in the morning, and the special observance began in the afternoon. First Jesus' betrayal by Judas and his death were commemorated. Then followed a commemoration of the Last Supper, which concluded with two celebrations of the Eucharist, one in the Martyrium, and the second, immediately after, by the cross erected on the rock identified as Golgotha, included within one corner of the Martyrium.

There was then time for a quick meal before two more services, in the Eleona and the Imbomon, commemorating again Christ's last teaching, and his arrest and trial. The congregation then went down the Mount of Olives to the site of the Agony, and on to Gethsemane. Back in the city, in the courtyard called Before the Cross, the trial before Pilate was commemorated. It was now early morning, and after a brief pause observances were resumed at Golgotha, with the veneration of the cross, the most treasured relic of the Jerusalem church. Three hours of gospel readings about the passion followed, and finally Christ's burial was commemorated in the Anastasis.

The Paschal Vigil began in the evening, with the Lucernarium, or service of light, the usual evening service, which began with the lighting of a lamp from the lamp burning perpetually in the cave of Christ's burial and resurrection. While the readings of the vigil proper were going on in the Martyrium, the catechumens were being baptized and confirmed, and about midnight were brought into the Martyrium to join the rest of the congregation for the Eucharist. Again, there were two celebrations of the Eucharist, one in the Martyrium and another immediately following in the Anastasis.

These special services were in addition to the normal daily services, which were augmented in any case during Lent. Egeria was struck by one particular characteristic of all the special observances: they were made up of antiphons, chants and readings appropriate to the time and the place. The Jerusalem church, living among the actual places connected with the last week of Christ's life, was able to commemorate the events of that week at the places where they took place, as well as at the time they happened. Its unique position enabled it to develop a series of observances, making of the Great Week an almost non-stop round of services and processions, enormously demanding on the participants, but affording them the opportunity of experiencing for themselves the passion, death and resurrection of Christ, the Passover sacrificed for us, and entering into his salvation, in the place where God in Christ reconciled humanity to himself. Yet although the earlier unitary celebration of the Christian Passover had come to be spread over a whole week, the developed Holy Week was not simply an historical commemoration, looking to the past. Initiation into the present experience of salvation was still there, and there was the expectation of its fulfillment in the final coming of Christ.

Later Developments

The observances of Jerusalem spread throughout the Church, and the Byzantine Holy Week services reflect many of the features described by Egeria. Away from Jerusalem, services were modified of necessity by the absence of the holy places, and the Jerusalem rite was adapted in various ways by different churches. One of the developments in the Christian East was of importance in shaping Holy Week as it came to be observed in the Byzantine rite, and as it is observed now in the Orthodox churches. In the course of several centuries the special services of the Jerusalem church were gradually merged with the regular daily services, so that in its final form the Liturgy of Holy Week in the Byzantine tradition contained strictly speaking no special services, but only the normal daily services, incorporating special elements proper to each day of the week. The West, on the other hand, retained a number of special observances, such as the palm procession, and the veneration of the cross, in addition to its regular services. The Western Easter Vigil began with the liturgical lighting and blessing of the new fire and Easter Candle, whereas the Byzantine rite had only an informal lighting of the people's candles from a light brought out of the sanctuary by the priest. Only in Jerusalem did the kindling of the new fire become one of the most dramatic features of the Easter Liturgy. Developments continued to take place until the end of the Middle Ages, and some of the distinctive features of Orthodox Holy Week belong to the latest stage of its development.

The Evolution of Lent

The period of instruction and fasting, with regular exorcism, which formed the final stage of a preparation for initiation lasting perhaps as long as three years, was the origin of the Lenten fast. Varying in length from three to six weeks, it came to be observed as a fast by other Christians out of devotion. By the fourth century the fast before the Christian Passover was generally observed throughout the Church, and in many places lasted for forty days, following the example of Jesus' forty days' fast in the desert after his baptism. Strictly speaking, it was made up of two elements, the six-day fast observed by all before Easter, and the additional weeks originating in the final preparation of the catechumens.

For some time after the establishment of Lent as a general observance its length and precise scope varied from church to church. East and West, represented by their leading churches, Constantinople and Rome, came to follow rather different principles in arriving at a final pattern for the period before Easter. Rome, whose pattern became that of the West, came to keep a fast of a total of forty days before Easter Day. Since Sunday was not included as a fast day, being the celebration of the resurrection, Lent came to consist of six weeks, each of six fasting days. This produced only thirty-six fasting days, and so in the seventh century four additional days were added, to make the number up to exactly forty. That meant that Lent, in Rome, began on a Wednesday, known as Ash Wednesday, and Roman practice became that of the whole West.

Constantinople, whose rite gradually became that of all the Orthodox churches, also kept a fast of forty days. But it did not include Holy Week in the total, regarding it as in some way distinct from Lent. Nor did it include Saturday as a fast day, except for the Saturday before Easter. But it did not exclude Saturdays and Sundays from the total, although they were not fasting days. It kept therefore a fast of six weeks, beginning on a Monday and ending on the Friday before Holy Week. That gave a total of thirty actual fasting days, out of the forty. But with Holy Week added, the total came to thirty-six days, as it had in Rome before the addition of four extra days.

11

The liturgical tradition of Constantinople, however, was greatly influenced by that of Jerusalem and Palestine. Palestinian Christians excluded Saturdays and Sundays from their calculation of the fast, and so kept an eight-week fast, including Holy Week, with five fasting days in each, to arrive at their forty days. Their Lent therefore lasted a week longer than that of Constantinople. Under Palestinian influence an eighth week, of modified fasting, was eventually added at Constantinople, probably in the early seventh century, and its observance gradually spread in the East.

Both in East and West, Lent, itself a preparation for Easter, acquired its own preparation. In Rome three Sundays came to be observed before Lent itself, Quinquagesima, Sexagesima and Septuagesima. Although not part of the fast itself, the period beginning with Septuagesima was marked by the use of purple vestments, and the disuse of the liturgical Alleluia. In Constantinople four Sundays came to lead into Lent. The Sunday immediately before Lent was observed as the Sunday of Forgiveness, and the three previous Sundays were added, one by one. Working backwards, they are the Sunday of the Last Judgment, the Sunday of the Prodigal Son, and the Sunday of the Tax Collector and the Pharisee. This last was added only in the eleventh century, so completing the pattern of Byzantine Lent, still observed by the Orthodox churches.

2

The Pattern of Orthodox Lent, Holy Week and Easter

The Triodion and Pentecostarion

The Triodion, containing the special texts for the Lenten period, begins with the Sunday of the Tax Collector and the Pharisee, and ends with the services of Holy Saturday. The Easter Vigil is the first of the services contained in the Pentecostarion, which provides the texts for the fifty days of Easter, concluding with Pentecost Sunday, the celebration of the coming of the Holy Spirit.

The Sundays before Lent

Four Sundays lead up to Lent. But even before the Sunday of the Tax Collector and the Pharisee, there is a preparatory note sounded in the gospel reading of the previous Sunday, which tells of Zacchaeus' eagerness to see Jesus as he passes by. The Church is reminded of the importance of a real desire to grow closer to Christ if our Lenten observances are to be of profit to us. The Sunday of the Tax Collector and the Pharisee calls us to humility and repentance, and the note of repentance is reinforced on the Sunday of the Prodigal Son. The danger of refusing to repent and lead a new life is emphasized by the Sunday of the Last Judgment. Finally the Sunday of Forgiveness reminds us both of our present state, by its commemoration of the expulsion of Adam from Paradise, and of the need for us to be forgiving, if we hope to receive God's forgiveness, and to be admitted once again to Paradise.

The Fast of Lent

The Lenten fast begins with Vespers on the Sunday of Forgiveness. The Orthodox Church has kept the Jewish custom of reckoning each day from sunset, and so the first service of each day is Vespers on what we should reckon the previous evening. Fasting is still taken seriously by Orthodox Christians—even if the strict rules, evolved by and for those leading the monastic life, are not usually fully observed by others—and there are frequent references to fasting in the texts of the Triodion. The fast is anticipated in the week beginning with the Sunday of the Last Judgment, which is also known as Cheese-fare Sunday, because after it no meat may be eaten until Easter Day. Once Lent itself begins, no meat or animal produce may be eaten on any day, except on the Feast of the Annunciation and on Palm Sunday, when fish is allowed. Wine and oil are also forbidden, except on Saturdays and Sundays, and certain feast days. The first week of Lent and Holy Week are in usual practice kept more strictly than the rest of Lent; and on Holy Friday and Holy Saturday as strict an observance as possible is encouraged.

The Pattern of Lent

Services throughout Lent and Holy Week follow the normal daily and weekly pattern. Vespers is followed by Compline; then comes the Midnight Office, and in the morning, Matins. A prominent part of Matins is the Canon, a poetic composition in nine odes, each ode of which is made up of a number of *troparia,* or short stanzas. In origin the Canon consisted of nine biblical canticles; and the troparia in origin were short refrains to the canticles appropriate to the day or feast. In time the canticles ceased to be used, except for the Magnificat at Matins, and during Lent. As purely poetic compositions, they came to constitute one of the richest elements in Orthodox worship, and provided a model for such devotional compositions as the Great Canon of St Andrew of Crete. The day itself is punctuated by the Hours, First, Third,

Sixth and Ninth, usually celebrated in conjunction with Vespers, Matins or the Liturgy. Together these services constitute the daily round of worship which evolved in monastic communities. In parish practice only the larger churches celebrate Vespers and Matins daily. In smaller parishes there might not be services each day, but only on Sundays and greater festivals. Sunday begins with Vespers on Saturday evening, combined in the Russian and some other Orthodox churches with Matins to form the All-night Vigil. In Greek practice, followed by other churches, Matins is celebrated in the morning, followed by the Liturgy, as the Eucharist is known in the Orthodox Church.

The Eucharist

The Orthodox Church has never made a general custom of celebrating the Liturgy daily, although in larger churches there may be a daily celebration. Saturdays and Sundays became the two days in the Christian East on which the Liturgy is regularly celebrated, together with major festivals which occur during the week. The Liturgy is held to be essentially a festive celebration, and the traditional Western distinction between sung and said celebrations is unknown in the East. That is why in Lent the Liturgy is not celebrated on the ordinary days of the fast. It is confined to Saturdays and Sundays, and the Feast of the Annunciation and Holy Thursday. But to make some provision for Holy Communion during Lent, there is celebrated on Wednesdays and Fridays, and on the first three days of Holy Week, the Liturgy of the Presanctified Gifts, at one time celebrated on all weekdays of Lent. This consists of Vespers, followed by Holy Communion from the sacrament consecrated at the previous celebration of the full Liturgy, and reserved for this purpose. Originally celebrated in the evening, towards the end of a day of complete abstinence from food and drink, it came to be celebrated earlier, perhaps in part to shorten the period of fasting. In contrast with Western practice, the Liturgy of the Presanctified Gifts is, at least since the 13th century, not celebrated on Holy Friday, the one day of the year when Holy Communion is given from the reserved sacrament as part of the Liturgy of the day in Roman Catholic and other churches. Of the two full eucharistic Liturgies in normal use among the Orthodox, that of St John Chrysostom is used on most occasions. That of St Basil the Great is used on ten days of the year, including the Sundays of Lent, except Palm Sunday, and Holy Thursday and Holy Saturday. They differ only in their eucharistic prayers, and certain other prayers, mostly still said in a low voice inaudible to the congregation.

The Sunday Themes

The themes of the Sundays in Lent were originally related to the final preparation of the catechumens for initiation at the Easter Vigil. In the course of time these themes were subordinated to others, and survive now largely only in the Scripture readings. The first Sunday in Lent came to commemorate the restoration of the icons in 843, after the long and bitter controversy in the East over the making and venerating of icons. In that year the decisions of the Seventh Ecumenical Council of 787 relating to icons were finally put into practice. The second came to commemorate St Gregory Palamas, renowned as the defender of the monks of Mount Athos and their way of praying in the so-called "hesychast controversy" in the fourteenth century. The third Sunday is devoted to a celebration of the victory of the cross, while St John of the Ladder, one of the most famous monastic teachers of the way to perfection, is commemorated on the fourth Sunday. The fifth Sunday is a commemoration of St Mary of Egypt, one of the great women ascetics of the Palestinian desert. These later commemorations, while overlaying the original themes of Lent, are not always inappropriate, and can be understood as forming a coherent pattern for the great fast.

Special Observances

Certain other days are of particular importance in Lent, and feature prominently in popular Orthodox devotion. In the first week of Lent, on the first four evenings, the Great Canon of St Andrew of Crete is used at Compline. Composed in the early seventh century and made up of nine canticles, it is an extended expression of repentance, drawing largely on biblical examples from Old and New Testaments. The refrain, "Have mercy on me, O God, have mercy on me," is repeated after each troparion. On the first four days of the first week of Lent it is chanted in four sections. On the Thursday of the fifth week the whole Canon is used at Matins.

Another important day is the Saturday of the fifth week, when the Acathist Hymn to the Mother of God is sung. Composed by Romanos the Melode in the sixth century, it came to be sung on the feast of the Annunciation, which was introduced some time in the middle of that century. Later the hymn, the most popular Eastern devotion to the Blessed Virgin Mary, was moved to the fifth Saturday in Lent, during which the feast almost always occurs. It brought with it a number of texts from the Annunciation to Vespers and Matins on that Saturday.

Holy Week and Easter

Between Lent, strictly reckoned, and Holy Week, stands the Saturday of Lazarus. It came to be closely linked with Palm Sunday in the Eastern tradition at least from the late fourth century, and the texts for each day contain a number of references to the other. They introduce the liturgical commemoration of the last days of Jesus' life, his death and his resurrection. Each day has its own themes, reflecting closely the gospel narratives. In Holy Week, as in the rest of Lent, the services follow the usual daily pattern, although in some of them the special elements predominate over their normal content. Orthodox Holy Week is still characterized by a peculiar feature, which it shared with the Roman Catholic Church until Rome began to renew its Holy Week services in the 1950s. From Palm Sunday evening until the end of the week almost all services are advanced by half a day, so that Matins of each day is celebrated the previous evening, and Vespers in the morning. This was the final result of a process which took place in the later Middle Ages, by which the evening services were gradually brought forward, perhaps in order to shorten the strict fast observed until after Vespers. So the original Easter Vigil, begun with Vespers on Holy Saturday evening, came to be celebrated on Saturday morning. Matins of Sunday, and the Easter Sunday Liturgy, were in turn advanced to fill the gap left, and begun at midnight, so becoming the present Easter Vigil.

The Epitaphion

Prominent in popular devotion on Holy Friday and Saturday is the part played by the *Epitaphion,* a large cloth on which is depicted the deposition of Christ. It is brought into the nave of the church from the sanctuary at the end of Vespers on Holy Friday, and set on a table or stand in the middle of the church, where it is venerated by the people. This is the equivalent of the veneration of the cross in Western practice. Towards the end of Matins of Holy Saturday, on Holy Friday evening, it is carried in procession round the outside of the church, representing the funeral procession of Christ. Replaced on its stand, it remains in the church until just before the Easter Vigil, when it is carried back into the sanctuary. Its use dates from as recently as perhaps the sixteenth century.

3

Sunday of the Tax Collector
and the Pharisee

The fourth Sunday before Lent is named after the gospel reading, Luke 18:1-14. The tax collector is taken as a model of humility, by contrast with the Pharisee, who is an example of pride. The Pharisee is presented as well-satisfied with himself, believing that he fulfills all that religion requires of him: he fasts twice a week, he gives tithes of all he owns. He despises the tax collector, who belongs to a class of people unpopular because of their profession and the collaboration it involved with the Roman authorities. But the tax collector is fully aware of his shortcomings. He knows he has no ground for boasting before God, and asks only for mercy: "God, be merciful to me, a sinner." But Jesus says that it was he who went home justified, not the Pharisee. For it was the tax collector who had received the grace of humility, and who is therefore the model for Christians.

From Vespers

My brothers and sisters,
let us not pray like the Pharisee;
for all who exalt themselves will be humbled.
But let us humble ourselves before God,
and fasting pray with the tax collector:
O God, be merciful to us sinners.

To you, the only Lord,
there came a Pharisee, ruled by vainglory,
and a tax collector, bowed down in repentance.
The first boasted,
and was deprived of good things;
the other stayed silent,
and was deemed fit to receive gifts.

19

Christ our God, by your love for us
strengthen me to make my own
his repentant groans.

All powerful Lord,
I know what tears can achieve:
for they brought Hezekiah up from death's door;
they rescued the sinful woman
from her many years' offenses;
they justified the tax-collector
rather than the Pharisee.
I pray you, number me with them,
and have mercy on me.

From Matins

Humility once exalted the tax collector,
who bewailed his sin
and cried: "Be merciful,"
and justified him.
Let him be our example,
for we have all fallen into the abyss of evil.
Let us cry to the Savior
from the bottom of our heart:
We have sinned, be merciful,
for you alone love us.

Brothers and sisters,
let us all humble ourselves,
and with groans and laments
strike our conscience; so that at the eternal judgment
we may be seen to be faithful and blameless,
obtaining forgiveness.
For there indeed is rest,
and we must pray now to see it;
there pain, grief, and sighing from the deep
are no more, in that marvelous Eden,
of which Christ is the maker,
for he is God,
together with the Father,
without beginning.

Lord, you condemned the Pharisee
who, boasting of his works,
justified himself.
You justified the tax collector
who, humbling himself,
with sorrowful sighing asked for mercy.
For you reject proud thoughts,
but do not despise contrite hearts.
So in humility we prostrate ourselves
before you, who suffered for us.
Grant us forgiveness and generous mercy.

Humility is the primary Christian virtue. It is often misunderstood as self-depreciation. Rather, it is a just assessment of oneself, based on accurate self-knowledge. Humility recognizes first that we are created beings, albeit in the image and likeness of God. It goes on to acknowledge that we are fallen creatures, in whom likeness to God has been obscured precisely by the pride which wants us to be independent of God. It then opens itself to receive the grace of Christ, who died to restore in us the likeness to God our pride had lost.

If in the gospel the tax collector is a model of humility, it is Christ himself who, in the Christian tradition, is the pattern for true humility:

[Christ] who, though he was in the form of God, emptied himself, taking the form of a slave, being born in human likeness. And being found in human form, he humbled himself, and became obedient to the point of death—even death on a cross. (Phil 2:6-7)

But the humility of Christ is only a reflection of the humility of God himself. That humility is shown first of all in creation: God wills to create creatures with whom he wishes to associate in love. But those creatures refuse his love, preferring to try to be like God themselves—paradoxically failing utterly, for their pride contrasts totally with his humility. God's humility is then shown again, for in Christ he becomes one of his own creatures, and on the cross gives himself totally in love, in order to heal human hearts of pride, and make us capable of sharing his own life. In God humility and love go closely together: what St Paul says about love in his famous hymn in 1 Corinthians 13 could equally well be said about humility.

Coming at the beginning of the pre-Lenten period, the Sunday of the Tax Collector and the Pharisee stresses that humility is the necessary basic condition for growth in the Christian life: it is the best protection from temptation, and the soil in which all the other virtues can take root and flourish. We receive it as we contemplate the humility of God in Christ, and desire to become as he is.

4

Sunday of the Prodigal Son

The parable of the Prodigal Son, Luke 15:11-32, read as the gospel on the third Sunday before Lent, is taken as a parable of the human condition. Through sin we have lost the close relationship with God we were created to enjoy as his sons and daughters. We have gone our own way, which has led us far from God, and our lives are impoverished. But we can return. Once we recognize the wretched state we are in, and long for something better, we have begun the journey home. God, like the father in the story, is looking out for us, longing for our return. When he sees us in the distance he runs to meet us, arms outstretched to welcome us back, with new clothes laid out for us and a party ready. The arms are those of God in Christ, stretched out for us on the cross: the party is the eternal life of the resurrection—the feast to which the Homily of St John Chrysostom will invite us on Easter night.

From Vespers

> I was entrusted with a land
> without sin and full of life,
> but I sowed it with sin,
> and with a sickle reaped the ears of idleness.
> I piled up in heaps
> the sheaves of my deeds,
> but did not spread them out
> on the threshing-floor of repentance.
> But I pray you, O our God,
> who have tilled the soil from all eternity,
> by your kind mercy's breeze blow away the chaff of my deeds,
> and grant me the harvest of forgiveness.
> Gather me up in your barn in heaven and
> save me.

Brothers and sisters,
let us discover the power of the mystery;
for the Father, good beyond measure,
goes to meet his dissolute son,
who runs back from sin to his father's house,
and puts his arms around him and kisses him.
He gives him again the marks of his family glory,
and mystically perfects the celebration on high,
sacrificing the fatted calf,
so that we might lead lives appropriate
to the one who sacrifices,
the Father who loves humankind,
and to him who is gloriously sacrificed,
the Savior of our souls.

The wealth given me by my father
I have wasted, and in misery
have fed with dumb animals.
I craved for their food,
but was faint with hunger,
unable to satisfy my appetite
But coming back to the merciful Father
I cry out with tears:
I prostrate myself before your love:
accept me as a hired hand,
and save me.

From Matins

Be quick to open for me a father's arms,
since I have spent my life dissolutely.
I look to the free riches of your mercy:
do not reject my impoverished heart.
For to you, Lord, I call with compunction:
I have sinned, save me.

Our Savior teaches us daily with his own voice,
so let us listen to the Scriptures,
as they tell of the prodigal son,
who came to his senses again.
Let us in faith reproduce his good repentance,

and in humility cry to God who knows all secrets:
Merciful Father, we have sinned before you
and do not deserve ever again
to be called your children,
as once we were.
But because your nature is always to love,
take me back and treat me
like one of your hired hands.

I have worshipped sensual pleasure,
complete wretch that I am,
and am totally enslaved
to passions' provocations.
I am alienated from you,
who love us.
But now I call with the prodigal's voice:
O Christ, I have sinned:
do not reject me, for only you are merciful.

Good Father, I have gone far from you.
But do not abandon me,
nor deprive me of your kingdom.
The most wicked enemy has stripped me
and taken away my wealth.
I have squandered dissolutely
all the spiritual gifts you gave me.

But now I have got up and come back to you
and I cry out:
Treat me like one of your hired hands.
For my sake on the cross
you opened wide your sinless hands,
to rescue me from the terrible wild beast
and reclothe me as I was before.
For mercy is with you alone.

The prodigal son is one of the scriptural models of repentance. Humbled by his experience, he turned away from his sin, and turned back towards God. In the Eastern spiritual tradition repentance plays a prominent part in the Christian life. Our sins are forgiven in baptism, but we continue to do wrong. Repentance is recognition of sin, condemnation of faults, and blaming oneself.

By themselves, these could lead to despair. But repentance is always undertaken in hope, because in the faith that by the cross all sins have been forgiven. It is both a change of heart, an inner conversion, and a practical change in one's behavior, leading to the practice of the virtues. That is why, with humility, it is a necessary condition for making any progress in the life of faith.

But these liturgical texts see in the Prodigal Son more than repentance: they speak of compunction—*penthos* in Greek. Repentance—*metanoia*—is personal and for specific sins. Compunction goes much further than repentance. It is a more general mourning or sadness for salvation lost, by oneself and by others. While repentance does not necessarily involve the emotions, compunction is a feeling, which expresses itself in tears. Tears play an important part in the Christian life in the Eastern tradition. They are a gift from God, and, like baptism, wash away sins. John Chrysostom said that a single tear extinguishes a brazier of faults and washes away the venom of sin. Compunction springs not only from a sense of salvation lost, but from fear of judgment. For though we may be forgiven after repenting of particular sins, we can never be sure that we shall not sin again; nor can we be certain of final victory over our faults.

Yet we can be certain of the unfailing love of God for us. St Luke's parable has been traditionally called the parable of the Prodigal Son: it could equally well be called that of the Loving Father. There is no sin that cannot be forgiven if we repent of it; and at the first sign of repentance the love of God is there to welcome the sinner home.

5

Saturday of the Dead

The second Sunday before Lent has as its theme the Last Judgment. In traditional Christian thought judgment and death are closely linked. In the Orthodox calendar the Saturday before the Sunday of the Last Judgment is observed as the Saturday of the Dead. This is perhaps the nearest Orthodox equivalent of All Souls' Day in the West, although commemoration of the departed is made every Saturday, and certain Saturdays in the year are particularly so observed.

From Vespers

Because of your resurrection from the dead,
O Christ, death no longer reigns
over those who die believers.
So we earnestly pray:
Give rest in your courts
and in the bosom of Abraham
to your servants who have served you in purity,
from Adam until now,
our fathers and brothers,
friends and relations,
everyone who has served faithfully in this life
in many different ways, O God,
and has passed over to you;
and deem them all fit
for your heavenly kingdom.

I lament and wail
when I think about death;
and see lying in the grave
our beauty, created in God's image,
deformed, dishonored, disfigured.

What marvel is this!
What mystery is this
that has happened to us?
Why is it we have been consigned to decay?
Why is it we have been linked with death?
In truth it is by the command of God,
who gives rest to the departed.

My beginning and the ground of my being
was your creative command.
For, wishing to make me a living being
out of what is seen and what is not seen,
you created my body from the earth,
and gave me a soul
by your divine and life-giving breath.
So, Savior, give rest to your servants
in the land of the living,
in the dwellings of the righteous.

From Matins

Give rest with your saints, O Christ,
to the souls of your servants,
where there is no pain or grief or groaning,
but life everlasting.

You alone are immortal,
who have made and formed human beings.
But we mortals have been formed from earth,
and to the same earth we shall go.
For you that made me commanded me and said:
"Earth you are and to earth you will return."
There will all we mortals go,
singing Alleluia as our funeral song.

Come, brothers and sisters, before the end,
and look at our clay,
and the weakness of our vile nature.
Consider our end,
and the organs of our fleshly vessel:
that human beings are dust,
food for worms, and decay;

that our bones are dry
and have no breath in them at all.
Look at the graves:
where is our glory,
where the beauty of our appearance,
where our eloquent speech,
where the eyebrow, and the eye?
All are dust and mere shadow.
So, Savior, spare us all.

Christ has risen,
freeing first-formed Adam from his bonds,
and destroying Hades' might.
Courage, all you dead,
for death is done to death,
and Hades too is stripped of strength.
Christ reigns, crucified and risen.
He has made our flesh imperishable.
He will raise us up,
and give us resurrection,
and make fit for that joyful glory
all who have put their trust in him,
with fervent steadfast faith.

The texts fully recognize human mortality and the reality of death and decay. At the same time they express the Christian sense that human beings are not meant simply to end in the grave: they are destined for eternal life with God. Death as we experience it is a consequence of sin, which distances us from God. But the death and resurrection of Jesus Christ have overcome the consequences of sin, including death, and have reconciled us to God, so opening the way to eternal life. Through faith and baptism we are incorporated into the risen life of Christ, and through the Holy Spirit we share already in his new life. We live in the hope of being raised to glory with him in the end.

But there is nothing automatic about our sharing in Christ's resurrection. We must put our faith into practice in the way we live, and must work with the Holy Spirit to restrain our vices and strengthen our virtues. We must pray always for God's mercy and his help, for ourselves and others. That prayer does not cease when we die, for our human relationships are not broken, only changed, by death. We pray for the departed because we still hold them in our love. For the Orthodox, prayer for the dead is a completely natural expression of our union in the risen Christ with those who have died.

The Orthodox Church does not have a clearly defined doctrine of what happens to us after death. But it prays for the dead in the faith that we continue to grow in our relationship with God after death. In the prayers of Pentecost it prays even for the salvation of those in hell, in the hope that the love of God may yet find a response even from those who so far have consistently rejected it. The Orthodox Church has no hesitation, either, in asking those who have died, in particular the saints, to pray for us, believing that they continue to hold us in their love, as we hold them in ours.

6

Sunday of the Last Judgment

In the Christian tradition a powerful motive for repentance is the prospect of judgment. Western Christians are used to reflecting on the Last Judgment in Advent, the season of four weeks immediately before Christmas. In the Orthodox Church the theme of judgment is one of the strands woven into the Lenten and pre-Lenten period, and into the services of Holy Week itself. This reflects the ancient Christian belief that the coming of Christ in judgment would take place during the Easter Vigil. The second Sunday before Lent is particularly devoted to the theme of judgment: the gospel at the Liturgy on this day is Matthew 25:31-46, the parable of the Sheep and the Goats, and it provides some of the images used in the liturgical texts. Others are drawn from the Book of Daniel and the Revelation to John.

From Vespers

> The trumpets will sound
> and the graves will be emptied,
> and all humankind will arise,
> quaking with fear.
> Those who have done good
> will joyfully rejoice,
> expecting to receive a reward.
> But those who have sinned will quake with fear,
> wailing terribly,
> sent to punishment
> and separated from the elect.
>
> I weep and wail
> when there come to mind
> the everlasting fire,
> the outer darkness,

the abyss of torment,
the fearful worm,
the ever-gnashing of teeth,
the ceaseless pain
coming to those who have sinned unceasingly,
who have provoked you to anger,
you, who abound in goodness.
I am one of them,
in my wretchedness the first.
But, compassionate judge,
in your mercy save me.

When the thrones are set in place
and the books opened,
and God sits in judgment,
what fear will there be!
When the angels stand in fear before you
and the stream of fire flows out,
what shall we do then,
we who must answer for many sins?
When we hear him calling
those blessed by the Father
into his kingdom,
but sending sinners to their punishment,
who shall endure this terrible sentence?
But you are the Savior
who alone loves humankind,
you are the king of the ages:
before the end comes
turn me by repentance,
and have mercy on me.

Since we know the Lord's commandments,
let us live accordingly:
let us give the hungry food,
the thirsty drink;
let us clothe the naked,
welcome strangers to our homes,
visit those in prison and the sick;
so that he who will judge the whole earth
will say even to us:

"Come, you that are blessed by my Father,
inherit the kingdom prepared for you."

From Matins

I think about that fearful day,
and bewail my evil deeds.
How shall I answer the immortal king?
How shall I, the prodigal,
dare to look at the judge?
Merciful Father,
only-begotten Son
and Holy Spirit,
have mercy on me.

What a time it will be,
and what a fearful day,
when the Judge will sit on his fearful throne!
Books will be opened
and deeds examined,
things hidden in darkness
will be made public.
Angels will run round,
gathering together all the nations.
Kings and rulers, slaves and free,
sinners and righteous, rich and poor,
come and listen:
because the Judge is coming
to judge the whole world.
Who will be able to stand before his face,
when the angels stand in his presence,
examining deeds, thoughts, and ideas,
whether of night or of day?
What a time it will be!
But before the end comes
let me speedily cry:
You, O God, alone are merciful,
make me repent and save me.

Orthodox Christians are reminded of the Last Judgment not
only by the verbal imagery of texts such as these. The scene is

depicted in the iconography of an Orthodox church, often in the narthex. Christ is shown enthroned at the top of the scene, a river of fire flowing from beneath his throne. On his left are the ranks of those condemned to eternal punishment, on his right those judged worthy of eternal life. Angels are blowing trumpets, the dead are being raised, and the righteous are entering Paradise, depicted in the bottom left hand corner of the composition. There Abraham holds righteous souls in his bosom, and the penitent thief stands, holding his cross.

The gospel for the Sunday of the Last Judgment makes clear the criterion by which we are and shall be judged. It is quite simply whether or not we have shown love to Christ in other people. Neither those rewarded nor those punished were aware of having done, or failed to do, anything for the Son of Man: so far as they knew, they had never come across him till that moment. But acts of kindness done, or left undone, for any of his brothers and sisters, are acts of kindness done, or left undone, for him. The commandments to love God, and to love our neighbor as ourselves, are inseparable, and in fulfilling the latter we also obey the former.

For all men and women are created in the image and likeness of God, and Christ, the perfect image of God, dwells in all of us. We find Christ in our neighbor, and not least in our neighbor who is in any kind of need. If Lent is a time when the thought of judgment should spur us to repentance, then authentic repentance leads us to put love into practice in our daily living and in all our relationships.

7

Sunday of Forgiveness:
The Expulsion of Adam From Paradise

The gospel read at the Liturgy, which gives its name to the Sunday immediately before Lent, is Matthew 6:14-21. It includes the warning that we shall be forgiven by God only if we are forgiving towards others. But the Sunday of Forgiveness is particularly associated with the ritual act of mutual forgiveness, which takes place after Vespers on Sunday evening, the first service of Monday, the first day of Lent. The main theme of the texts at Vespers and Matins, however, is not forgiveness but the expulsion of Adam from Paradise. It is because of Adam's sin, the sin of all humankind, that we need God's forgiveness—the forgiveness we can receive only if we ourselves are forgiving to one another. The texts for this Sunday are inspired by the early chapters of Genesis. There are hints, too, of the parable of the Prodigal Son.

From Vespers

> The Lord who formed me
> took clay from the ground
> and by life-giving breath
> he gave me a soul
> and I became a living being.
> He honored me and gave me dominion on earth
> over all that can be seen,
> and made me dwell with angels.
> But the deceiver Satan,
> by means of the serpent,
> enticed me by food.
> He drew me away from God's glory;
> he handed me over to earth

and to the abyss of death.
But, Lord, in your compassion
call me back again.

Adam sat opposite Paradise.
He bewailed his nakedness and wept:
"How unhappy I am,
by evil deceit persuaded and misled,
and removed far from glory!
How unhappy I am,
in simplicity stripped naked,
and now in need!
No more, O Paradise,
shall I rejoice in your delights;
no more shall I see my Lord
and God and Creator;
for I shall return to the ground
from which I was taken.
I cry to you, Lord,
merciful and compassionate:
I have fallen,
have mercy on me."

Adam was driven out of Paradise
because he ate from a tree.
Sitting opposite he cried aloud,
and with pitiful voice uttered this lament:
"How unhappy I am!
How great is my suffering,
wretch that I am!
One command of the Lord I disobeyed,
and for that I have been deprived
of every blessing.
Paradise most holy,
for my sake planted
and closed because of Eve,
pray to your Creator and my Maker,
that I may enjoy your blossom to the full."
Then the Savior said to him:
"I do not desire the loss
of the creature I formed,

but that he should be saved
and come to the knowledge of the truth.
For he who comes to me
I will not drive away."

From Matins

Exiled once, Lord, from Paradise
because of food taken from a tree,
you have brought us back again
by your cross and passion,
my Savior and my God.
By that cross strengthen us
to keep the fast in holiness
and, by the prayers of your Mother,
to venerate your divine resurrection,
the Passover of salvation.

Adam was driven out of Paradise
because disobedient he had eaten food;
to Moses was given the vision of God,
because by fasting
he had purified his spiritual sight.
So if we yearn to inhabit Paradise
we should abstain from unprofitable food;
if we would see God,
we should fast like Moses forty days.
Persevering sincerely
in prayer and intercession,
we should still our spiritual passions,
put to flight our bodies' lusts.
Lightly we should set out
on the way to heaven.
There the choirs of angels never cease
to praise the undivided Trinity.
There we shall see
the incomparable beauty of the Lord.
Son of God, giver of life,
you are our hope:
make us fit to rejoice

> with the hosts of angels,
> through the prayers of your Mother, O Christ,
> and those of the apostles, martyrs
> and all the saints.

The picture of Adam, the figure of humanity, bewailing the loss of his intimacy with God and all the delights of Paradise, is the appropriate background against which Lent is set. For the Lenten pilgrimage is precisely the return journey to Paradise, whose gates are opened again for the human race by the cross of Christ. "Truly, I say to you, today you will be with me in Paradise," says Jesus in St Luke's Gospel (23:43) from the cross to the penitent thief crucified alongside him. We have seen how the iconography of the Last Judgment includes the thief already in Paradise, holding his cross.

The Ceremony of Forgiveness

After Vespers there is the ceremony of forgiveness. The priest stands next to the icon stand, on which is the icon of the day. Members of the congregation come up in turn to kiss the icon, and to prostrate themselves in front of the priest. They ask his forgiveness with the words: "Forgive me, a sinner." Then the priest asks their forgiveness, prostrating himself before them, and blesses them. Members of the congregation may then go to their fellow Christians, each asking forgiveness of the other.

This formal act of mutual forgiveness enacts Christ's injunction, given in the gospel at the Liturgy earlier in the day. By giving and accepting forgiveness from each other, Christians prepare themselves to receive God's forgiveness. Truly to forgive is one of the most difficult ways of expressing Christian love; and accepting forgiveness is one of the hardest forms of Christian humility. Few better ways of beginning the observance of Lent could be devised than this. Forgiving, and accepting forgiveness, are ways of taking up the cross Christ commands us to carry. They are also ways of entering into the new life of the resurrection.

This truth of the Christian life is made clear during the ceremony of forgiveness, when the choir sings quietly some of the Easter hymns. The goal of the Lenten fast is present in its beginning, and the fast is undertaken in the sure hope that the cross of Christ has already won the victory over human sinfulness. The prodigal who demonstrates his repentance by observing Lent sincerely will without doubt be welcomed by Christ on Easter Day, and be numbered among the righteous at the Last Judgment.

8

First Week of Lent:
The Great Canon

The texts for the first week of Lent combine a number of themes. Fasting from food goes hand in hand with fasting from the passions. The fast is also a time of spiritual combat, as we struggle to restrain vice and cultivate virtue. Human sin and God's mercy on those who repent are prominent. The suffering and death of Jesus, and the power of the cross to save and give new life are recurrent themes, and echoes of the Prodigal Son and the expulsion of Adam from Paradise are heard.

In popular devotion the first week of Lent is dominated by the Great Canon of St Andrew of Crete. Composed in the first half of the eighth century, this penitential hymn consists of nine canticles. It ranges widely over the Scriptures of both Old and New Testaments, drawing on examples of sinners and saints in order to urge its hearers to repentance, and to express their sorrow for sin. In the first week of Lent each canticle is divided into four, and one section is sung each evening from Monday to Thursday at Great Compline. On the Thursday of the fifth week of Lent the whole Canon is sung at Matins.

At all weekday services during Lent the Prayer of St Ephrem is said:

Lord and Master of my life,
keep far from me the spirit of futility,
discouragement, lust for power, and empty speech.
Grant to your servant the spirit of chastity,
humility, patience and love.
Yes, my Lord and king, grant me to see my own sins
and not to judge my neighbor.
For you are blessed for ever. Amen.

After each of the three sentences a prostration is made. On some occasions there follows the prayer "O God, cleanse me, a sinner," said twelve times with a bow after each repetition. The whole prayer is then repeated, with a single prostration at the end.

From Vespers on Sunday

> Begin the fast with joy,
> prepare for spiritual battle.
> Cleanse the soul,
> purify the flesh.
> Abstain, as from food,
> so from every passion,
> indulging in the Spirit's virtues.
> Persevere in them passionately:
> so shall we all be reckoned fit
> to witness the passion and death
> of Christ our God,
> and his holy Passover,
> rejoicing in spirit.

> Your grace, Lord, has shone out,
> the light of our souls has shone out.
> See, now is the acceptable time;
> See, now is the time of repentance.
> Let us then put off the works of darkness
> and put on the armor of light;
> that we may cross the fast's great ocean
> and come to the resurrection on the third day
> of our Lord and Savior Jesus Christ,
> who saves us.

From Vespers on Tuesday

> Let us keep the fast,
> not abstaining from food alone,
> but banishing all bodily passions;
> that we may enslave the tyrant flesh
> and be made fit to share in the Lamb,
> the Son of God, willingly slaughtered

for the sake of the world.
May we celebrate spiritually
the Savior's resurrection from the dead.
Exalted on high
and radiant in virtues,
by our noble actions
we shall rejoice the heart
of him who loves humankind.

From Vespers on Wednesday

Keeping the fast bodily,
brothers and sisters,
let us keep it spiritually as well.
Let us undo the bonds of wickedness,
tear up imposed contracts that ensnare,
cancel all unjust agreements,
give bread to the hungry
and bring into our house
the homeless poor,
so that we may receive
from Christ our God
abundant mercy.

From Vespers on Thursday

How great is the power of your cross!
It has caused abstinence
to flourish in the Church,
plucking out by the roots
Adam's sinful greed in Eden.
That brought death to mortals,
but the cross, incorrupt,
pours out on the world immortality,
like a new river from Paradise,
by the stream of your life-giving blood
mixed with water.
By it all things are made alive.
By it sweeten for us the fast,
O God of Israel, great in mercy.

From the Great Canon of St Andrew of Crete

From Canticle One

It is time to repent.
I come to you, my Creator.
Remove from me the burden of sin,
and in your compassion
grant me forgiveness.

Savior, do not reject me,
do not thrust me from you.
Remove from me the burden of sin,
and in your compassion
grant me forgiveness.

Savior, forgive all my offenses,
intentional or unintentional,
open or secret,
known or unknown.
For you are God,
have mercy and save me.

Savior, from my earliest days
I have rejected your laws,
I have been dominated by passions.
Throughout my life
I have been careless and idle.
That is why I cry to you, Savior,
now the end has come:
Save me!

From Canticle Two

Look and see that I am God,
who once for my people
rained down manna
and brought water from the rock
in the desert,
by my right hand alone
and by my own might.

"Look and see that I am God":
let me hear the Lord
when he calls,
give up my former sin
and let me fear him
as judge and God.

I have been wounded,
I have been beaten.
Look, here are the hostile weapons
which have gone through my soul and body.
Look, here are the wounds,
the sores, the injuries:
I cry out to you—
see the stripes inflicted by
passions willingly indulged.

Know and see
that I am God.
I search hearts,
punish thoughts,
reprove actions,
burn up sins;
I protect the orphan,
the humble and the poor.

From Canticle Three

Establish, Lord, on the rock
of your commandments
my unstable heart:
for you only are holy
and Lord.

I have gained
as the source of life
you, death's destroyer.
Before the end
I call out to you
from my heart:
I have sinned,
have mercy on me
and save me.

Have mercy, Lord,
I cry to you for mercy,
when you come with your angels
to pay back everyone
for what they have done.

The prayer of those who praise you,
Lord, do not reject,
but be merciful, for you love humankind,
and forgive those
who pray to you in faith.

From Canticle Four

I have sullied my body,
I have besmirched my spirit,
and I am wounded all over.
But as a doctor, O Christ,
heal my body and spirit for me
through repentance.
Wash and purify me,
and make me clean, O my Savior,
make me whiter than snow.

When you were crucified, O Word,
you offered your body and blood
on behalf of all:
your body to refashion me,
your blood to wash me clean.
You gave up your spirit, O Christ,
to bring me to your Father.

A very wealthy man and upright,
with much money and many cattle,
dressed like a king in purple
and wearing a crown,
Job suddenly became a beggar,
stripped of wealth, reputation,
and royal status.

If one who was upright and blameless
more than all others
did not escape the snares and traps

of the deceiver,
what shall I do,
wretched and sinful as I am,
when some sudden misfortune happens to me?

The services of Lent contain Orthodox teaching about the ascetic life. The reality of human sinfulness is fully acknowledged. At the same time the essential freedom of the human will is implicitly asserted: it is possible not to sin, if we really want to. Salvation is the result of God's graciousness, demonstrated on the cross, and of our own effort to obey the commandments. The Orthodox tradition uses the word "synergy," cooperation, to speak of the way in which we work together with God to overcome sin in our life.

There is no suggestion that we can earn our salvation: it is God's free gift. But the Christian East never experienced the controversy between Augustine and Pelagius about free will, and so has never had to define the role of free will in relation to God's grace. It has continued to think and speak about salvation in the same way as the early Church: it is God who saves us, and we cannot save ourselves. Yet we must be willing to accept what God offers, and to work with him to the fullest extent of which we are capable. So at the beginning of Lent we are reminded of the need, not only to repent, but to show the reality of our repentance by disciplining ourselves to lead a new life.

9

First Sunday of Lent:
The Sunday of Orthodoxy

L ent was in origin the time of final preparation for candidates for baptism at the Easter Vigil, and this is reflected in the readings at the Liturgy, today and on all the Sundays of Lent. But that basic theme came to be subordinated to later themes, which dominated the hymnography of each Sunday. The dominant theme of this Sunday since 843 has been that of the victory of the icons. In that year the iconoclastic controversy, which had raged on and off since 726, was finally laid to rest, and icons and their veneration were restored on the first Sunday in Lent. Ever since, that Sunday has been commemorated as the "triumph of Orthodoxy."

Orthodox teaching about icons was defined at the Seventh Ecumenical Council of 787, which brought to an end the first phase of the attempt to suppress icons. That teaching was finally re-established in 843, and it is embodied in the texts sung on this Sunday.

From Vespers

> Inspired by your Spirit, Lord,
> the prophets foretold your birth
> as a child incarnate of the Virgin.
> Nothing can contain or hold you;
> before the morning star
> you shone forth eternally
> from the spiritual womb of the Father.
> Yet you were to become like us
> and be seen by those on earth.
> At the prayers of those your prophets
> in your mercy reckon us fit
> to see your light,

for we praise your resurrection,
holy and beyond speech.

Infinite, Lord, as divine,
in the last times
you willed to become incarnate
and so finite;
for when you took on flesh
you made all its properties your own.
So we depict the form
of your outward appearance
and pay it relative respect,
and so are moved to love you;
and through it we receive the grace of healing,
following the divine traditions of the apostles.

The grace of truth has shone out;
the things once foreshadowed
now are revealed in perfection.
See, the Church is decked
with the embodied image of Christ,
as with beauty not of this world,
fulfilling the tent of witness,
holding fast the Orthodox faith.
For if we cling to the icon
of him whom we worship,
we shall not go astray.
May those who do not so believe
be covered with shame.
For the image of him who became human
is our glory:
we venerate it,
but do not worship it as God.
Kissing it, we who believe cry out:
O God, save your people,
and bless your heritage.

We have moved forward
from unbelief to true faith,
and have been enlightened
by the light of knowledge.
Let us then clap our hands like the psalmist,

and offer praise and thanksgiving to God.
And let us honor and venerate
the holy icons of Christ,
of his most pure Mother,
and of all the saints,
depicted on walls, panels and sacred vessels,
setting aside the unbelievers' ungodly teaching.
For the veneration given to the icon
passes over, as Basil says, to its prototype.
At the intercession of your spotless Mother,
O Christ, and of all the saints,
we pray you to grant us your great mercy.

We venerate your icon, good Lord,
asking forgiveness of our sins,
O Christ our God.
For you freely willed
in the flesh to ascend the cross,
to rescue from slavery to the enemy
those whom you had formed.
So we cry to you with thanksgiving:
You have filled all things with joy,
our Savior, by coming to save the world.

The name of this Sunday reflects the great significance which icons possess for the Orthodox Church. They are not optional devotional extras, but an integral part of Orthodox faith and devotion. They are held to be a necessary consequence of Christian faith in the incarnation of the Word of God, the Second Person of the Trinity, in Jesus Christ. They have a sacramental character, making present to the believer the person or event depicted on them. So the interior of Orthodox churches is often covered with icons painted on walls and domed roofs, and there is always an icon screen, or iconostasis, separating the sanctuary from the nave, often with several rows of icons. No Orthodox home is complete without an icon corner, where the family prays.

Icons are venerated by burning lamps and candles in front of them, by the use of incense and by kissing. But there is a clear doctrinal distinction between the veneration paid to icons and the worship due to God. The former is not only relative, it is in fact paid to the person represented by the icon. This distinction safeguards the veneration of icons from any charge of idolatry.

Although the theme of the victory of the icons is a secondary one on this Sunday, by its emphasis on the incarnation it points us to the basic Christian truth that the one whose death and resurrection we celebrate at Easter was none other than the Word of God who became human in Jesus Christ.

10

Second Sunday of Lent:
St Gregory Palamas

Just as the first Sunday in Lent came to be celebrated as the triumph of Orthodoxy, its original theme overlaid by a later historical one, so the second Sunday in Lent came in 1368 to be the commemoration of St Gregory Palamas.

This gives the Orthodox calendar a certain coincidental link with that of the Roman Catholic Church, which on the second Sunday in Lent commemorates the transfiguration of Jesus. St Gregory, who became Archbishop of Thessalonica, was prominently involved in a dispute in the fourteenth century which arose over certain ascetic practices on Mount Athos. It concerned the claim of some of the Athonite monks to be able to see the divine glory with their physical sight while praying. Gregory defended the monks against theological attacks made on them, and his position was upheld by two local Councils, held in Constantinople in 1347 and 1351. The monks' claim to see the same glory which was revealed to the disciples at the transfiguration was vindicated.

The theme of today's hymns is largely praise of St Gregory for his defense of Orthodoxy. But an older theme of the day was that of the Prodigal Son, embodied in a canon still sometimes used at Matins, in addition to one in honor of Gregory.

From Vespers

> Your tongue is awake to teach,
> it resounds in our hearts' hearing,
> and rouses sluggish souls.
> Your God-spoken words are a ladder
> carrying heavenwards those on earth.

So, Gregory, marvel of Thessaly,
pray ceaselessly to Christ to
illuminate with divine light
those who honor you.

From Matins

Making our own the prodigal's words,
with hot tears we fall before you,
Father and God of all, and cry,
We have sinned,
we have gone away from you,
and become slaves to lust.
But accept our repentance.

Sinning on earth,
I am terrified of heaven.
For I must be reproved at the judgment,
when all will stand before you, O Word,
judged by your just judgment.

Now has come the time to work:
at the door stands the judge.
Let us arise and fast,
offering tears of shame,
joined with almsgiving,
as we cry out:
Our sins are more
than the sand of the sea.
But set us free,
Creator of all,
for imperishable crowns.

The Word who is without beginning
with the Father and the Spirit
is born of the Virgin
who knew not a man,
passing the law of nature.
He remained what he was,
and has remained
in that which he took from us.
For he is one Son in two natures,

preserving all that is distinctive
both of divinity and humanity.

Your younger son was I,
and I have squandered your wealth,
by leading an evil life.
I have lost what you gave me
and have deprived myself of your goodness.
So I come to you, Father and God,
asking your forgiveness.

Our dying nature you have revived,
Virgin Mother of God,
for you alone have given life birth.
That is why we who believe
acknowledge you to be our salvation,
since you have brought forth
as a human being
the God of our fathers.

From Vespers on Sunday Evening

Astray on the mountains
of fearful transgressions,
look for me, O Word;
call me back to you again,
and drive far from my mind
all its evil habits.
Restore me to life from death,
and purify me by fasting,
for in tears I call out to you,
Lord Christ, have compassion on me
for your mercy's sake,
great and abundant.

At the start of the third week
of the fast,
let us who believe
praise the Holy Trinity
and with joy spend
the time that is left.
Putting to death our fleshly passions

> let us gather divine flowers,
> to weave wreaths
> for the queen of days,
> so that, wearing wreaths,
> we may all praise Christ as victor.

The glory that was revealed at Christ's transfiguration is in Orthodox teaching the uncreated light of the Holy Spirit, the light of divinity. Shining momentarily then, it was to be fully revealed in the resurrection of Jesus. It is the same glory that will be revealed at the coming of Christ to judge the world and establish finally the kingdom of God. By that glory we are all destined to be transfigured, and not only we, but the whole of creation. We can begin to share in it in this life, for the grace of the Holy Spirit, and so God himself, lives within us from our baptism. Yet although we really share in the life of God, we remain creatures, fundamentally different from God our Creator. The Eastern Christian tradition had long affirmed both these apparently conflicting truths by distinguishing between the essence of God, which we can never know, and his energies, in which we can share. The latter are no less God, for they are consubstantial with his essence. This distinction, preserving both God's transcendence and his immanence, became formal Orthodox teaching in the fourteenth century.

Prayer and a disciplined Christian life are the ways by which we can grow in the Holy Spirit, and so be progressively changed by the Spirit "from glory to glory" (2 Cor 3:17-18). Just as Jesus is raised to the glory of the resurrection because he willingly suffers death, so we must pass through death to our fallen, sinful selves in order to be raised with him to the glory of God's kingdom. The Lenten pilgrimage is the road to glory.

11

Third Sunday of Lent: Sunday of the Cross

In the West the veneration of the cross came to be part of the Good Friday Liturgy. It has always remained such in the Roman Catholic Church, and now has a place in the Liturgy of the Church of England. There is no veneration of the cross as such on Good Friday in most Orthodox churches, although the representation of the dead Christ, the Epitaphios, figures prominently in Orthodox devotion on that day. But the Orthodox Church does commemorate the cross half-way through Lent. Towards the end of Matins on the third Sunday in Lent a cross is brought into the nave of the church in solemn procession, and placed in the center of the church. It is censed, and the cross is venerated by clergy and people, who prostrate themselves in front of the cross before kissing it. The cross remains in church throughout the week, and is venerated after each service:

> We venerate your cross, O Lord,
> and glorify your holy resurrection.

From Vespers

> Hail! life-giving cross,
> invincible banner
> of pure religion,
> gate of paradise,
> strength of believers,
> defense of the Church.
> By you the curse
> has been undone, destroyed,
> the power of death devoured,
> and we have been raised

from earth to heaven.
Unbeatable weapon,
demonic powers' foe,
martyrs' glory,
boast of holy monks,
salvation's harbor,
from you the world
receives great mercy.

When all creation saw you,
all things' Maker and Creator,
hang naked on the cross,
it was changed by fear
and wailed.
The sun's light failed
and the earth quaked.
The rocks were rent,
the veil of the temple torn in two.
The dead were raised from their tombs,
and the powers of heaven
cried out in astonishment:
How amazing this is!
The judge is judged,
he wills to suffer death,
to heal and renew the world.

From Matins

The flaming sword no longer guards
the gate of Eden;
it has been strangely quenched
by the wood of the cross.
Death's sting and hell's victory
have been struck down.
For you, my Savior, have come
calling to those in hell:
Come back again to Paradise!

Come, let us who have faith
venerate the life-giving wood,
on which Christ the king of glory

willed to open wide his arms.
He raised us up to our former happiness,
we whom once the enemy
led astray through pleasure,
and made exiles from God.
Come, let us who have faith
venerate the wood
by which we have been reckoned fit
to strike the heads
of our unseen enemies.
Come, all peoples and nations,
let us honor the Lord's cross in song.

Rejoice, O cross,
perfect ransom of fallen Adam.
In you our faithful kings gloried,
and by your power they mightily subdued
the people of Ishmael.
We Christians now kiss you with godly fear,
and the God who was nailed to you
we glorify as we cry out:
O Lord, crucified on the cross,
have mercy on us,
for you are good
and love the human race.

Today the ruler of creation
and Lord of glory
is nailed to the cross
and his side pierced.
He, the Church's sweetness,
tastes gall and sour wine.
He is crowned with thorns
who decks the heaven with clouds.
With mocking robe is he dressed,
and by hand of clay is struck
him who formed man with his hands.
He is struck on the back
who robes the heaven in clouds.
He is spat on and flogged,
insulted and battered.

> To all this my rescuer and God
> submits for my sake,
> condemned as I am,
> so that from its error
> he may save the world,
> for he is compassionate.

The Sunday of the Holy Cross is the Orthodox equivalent of the fourth Sunday in Lent in the traditional Western calendar, which had the popular name of Refreshment Sunday. The *synaxarion* for the Sunday of the Cross explains that:

> Inasmuch as in the forty days of fasting we in a way crucify ourselves...and become bitter and despondent and failing, the life-giving cross is presented to us for refreshment and assurance, for remembrance of our Lord's passion, and for comfort...We are like those following a long and cruel path, who become tired, see a beautiful tree with many leaves, sit in its shadow and rest for a while and then, as if rejuvenated, continue their journey; likewise today, in the time of fasting and difficult journey and effort, the life-giving cross was planted in our midst by the holy fathers to give us rest and refreshment, to make us light and courageous for the remaining task. (Quoted from Alexander Schmemann, *Great Lent*, p. 77)

Every Sunday of the year is a celebration of the resurrection of Christ, more explicitly so in Orthodox liturgical texts than in Western. In Lent too at Matins troparia from the Canon of the Resurrection are sung. But on this Sunday the resurrection resounds more loudly than usual, for the *irmoi*, the opening troparia of each ode of the canon, are those of the Easter canon. Easter hymns were sung on the Sunday of Forgiveness, immediately before Lent began: they are sung again now halfway through Lent. This is a particularly striking instance of the way in which Orthodoxy never separates Christ's death and resurrection: it is the cross that brings new life, and new life cannot be had without death. So today's texts concentrate not on the sufferings of Christ, but on the new life and renewal which his death gives to us and to all creation. The cross is life-giving, because the one who died on it is himself the Creator and source of life.

That is why, in the Orthodox tradition, the cross is above all the sign of victory, God's victory over sin and death. It is carried by the triumphant Christ in Hades in the icon of Easter. It opens the way to Paradise, from which we are in exile because of our sin, and is nothing less than cosmic in the scope of its healing and renewing power.

12

Fourth Sunday of Lent: St John of the Ladder

St John of the Ladder, or Climacus, is so called because of his book *The Ladder to Paradise*. He was a monk of the monastery of St Catherine at Mount Sinai in the seventh century. His book, which became very popular in the East, is about the thirty stages by means of which Christians can reach moral perfection. His commemoration on the fourth Sunday in Lent, though a later addition, fits well with the Lenten theme of the moral and spiritual discipline required of a Christian: John is a model ascetic, and in monasteries his book is appointed for Lenten reading.

Some of the texts are on another theme. The first canon at Matins in the Triodion is based on the parable of the Good Samaritan, Luke 10:30-37. The Christian, wounded by sin, is compared with the man who fell among thieves; the Good Samaritan is Christ himself, who comes to heal us.

From Vespers on Saturday Evening

> Holy father John,
> your mouth has indeed
> always proclaimed God's praise.
> In your great wisdom
> you have devoted yourself
> to the Scriptures inspired by God
> which train us in righteousness.
> Enriched with the grace
> drawn from them,
> you have become blessed,
> and overturned the plans
> of all the ungodly.

Glorious father John,
you purified your soul
with the streams of your tears.
By your vigils through the night
you have obtained God's favor,
and have been raised,
blessed as you are,
to his love and beauty;
in which you now rightly take delight,
ever rejoicing, devout and holy father,
with all your fellow athletes for Christ.

From Matins

I have become, O Christ,
like the man who fell
into the hands of robbers,
and was left half dead by their blows.
So I have been wounded,
Savior, by my own sins.

Traveling on life's way, O Christ,
I have been severely injured by thieves
because of my passions.
But raise me up, I pray.

My passions have stripped me
of your commandments,
Christ my Savior,
and I have been injured by pleasures.
But pour your mercy on me.

When the priest and Levite saw me,
it was clear they could not help,
for they passed me by.
But you in your mercy
have now given me salvation
and brought me to safety.

My restless thoughts
have robbed my mind,
they have wounded me

by my passions
and left me for dead
in my many sins.
But, Savior, heal me.

By my thievish thoughts,
O Savior, I have ruined my life,
beaten by my sins.
So I have been stripped,
O God, of your divine image,
you who love humankind.
But have mercy on me.

Come, let us work in the vineyard of the spirit,
and make the fruits of repentance grow in it:
not working hard for food and drink,
but by prayer and fasting
bringing virtues to perfection.
Then the Lord of the vineyard will be pleased,
and will provide the wage,
by which he redeems us from the debt of sin,
he who alone is merciful.

From Vespers on Sunday

Let us who believe
make great efforts
in this time of the fast
to practice self-control,
so that we may receive great praise,
and by the mercy of our great God and king
be delivered from the flames of hell.

Past the half-way mark of the fast,
let us clearly display
the first signs of divine glory,
and speed on eagerly to reach
the goal of a virtuous life,
so that we may receive
the joy that never fades.

Adam fell into the hands
of thieving thoughts.

His mind was robbed,
his inmost self wounded.
He lay naked without help.
The priest who came before the Law
took no notice of him;
the Levite who came after the Law
did not even look at him.
You alone helped him, O God,
who came not from Samaria
but from the Mother of God.
Glory to you!

The texts in honor of John speak of his ascetic life and the grace he thereby gained. The Orthodox tradition knows no opposition or contrast between God's grace and our own efforts to lead a good life. It takes for granted that we have to struggle hard to discipline faults and cultivate virtues. For although human nature is wounded, it is not completely helpless. The Orthodox tradition has a less pessimistic view of human nature than some Western traditions, which lay great stress on human corruption. It is true that we are gravely wounded, and unable to heal ourselves: we are like the man who fell into the hands of robbers in Luke's parable of the Good Samaritan. We need someone to help us up, and provide us with the means of healing, as the Samaritan came to the rescue of the man who was attacked by thieves. In the early Church, the Samaritan was often understood as a figure of Christ himself, who comes to bind up and heal the wounds inflicted by human sin. We cannot heal ourselves: only God can save us. Yet we ourselves must fight against our sinful impulses as hard as we can. Lent is about both our ascetic struggle and God's healing grace, strengthening us and enabling us to grow towards perfection.

13

Thursday of the Great Canon

Vespers, on Wednesday evening, is part of the Liturgy of the Presanctified Gifts, and is usually anticipated in the morning. It includes echoes of the parable of the Good Samaritan and of the Prodigal Son.

Thursday Matins is normally anticipated on Wednesday evening, and includes the whole of the Great Canon of St Andrew of Crete. In preparation for the commemoration of St Mary of Egypt on Sunday, another Canon is read in her honor, and her Life, written by Sophronius, Patriarch of Jerusalem, is read in the course of the service. Two short Canons of the Apostles are also read.

From Vespers

Wretch that I am,
I have fallen into the hands of robbers—
my own thoughts.
My mind has been stripped,
and I have been severely beaten.
My whole being is wounded,
and stripped of virtues
I lie naked on life's road.
The priest saw me in sharp pain,
but thought my wounds incurable.
He took no notice of me,
refusing to look at me.
The Levite could not bear my agony,
destructive of my very being,
and when he saw me
passed by on the other side.
But you, Christ my God,
were pleased to come incarnate,

not from Samaria but from Mary.
In your great love for us,
give me healing
and pour your abundant mercy on me.

From the Great Canon of St Andrew of Crete

From Canticle Eight

Just Judge and Savior,
have mercy on me
and rescue me from the fire
and from the threat of punishment
I must face, justly deserved,
at the Judgment.
Forgive me before the end,
through virtue and repentance.

Like the robber I call out:
"Remember me!"
Like Peter I weep bitterly;
like the tax collector I call out,
"Forgive me, Savior."
I weep like the prostitute.
Hear my wailing,
as once you heard
the Canaanite woman's.

Heal, Savior, the festering wound
of my humble soul,
for you are the only doctor.
Apply a poultice,
pour on oil and wine:
acts of repentance,
compunction with tears.

Like the Canaanite woman I shout:
"Have mercy on me, Son of David."
Like the woman with a hemorrhage,
I touch the fringe of your clothes.
I weep as Martha and Mary
wept for Lazarus.

From Canticle Nine

From seedless conception
inexplicable birth;
of husbandless mother
pregnancy chaste.
For the birth that is God's
makes all creatures new.
So all generations
rightly magnify you,
Mother wedded of God.

My mind is damaged,
my body become weak,
my speech has failed,
my life has died; the end is at the door.
What then shall I do,
when the Judge comes
to examine what I have done?

I have set before myself
Moses' account of the world's creation,
and then all the canonical Scriptures
that tell me the story
of the just and the wicked.
But I have imitated the wicked,
not the just: I have sinned against God.

The law has no power,
the gospel makes no impact,
and I take no notice
of any of the Scriptures:
the prophets are of no avail,
nor any word of the Just One.
My wounds have increased
since there is no doctor to cure me.

I set before myself
examples from the New Testament,
to move me to compunction.
So imitate the just,
ignore the sinful;
and propitiate Christ
by prayer and fasting,
chastity and gravity.

From Vespers on Thursday

> Nailed, Lord, to the cross,
> you tore up Adam's record
> with the divine spear.
> Wherefore, O Word,
> tear off my bonds,
> that I may rejoice
> to offer you in faith
> the sacrifice of praise;
> for I have found
> the acceptable time of the fast,
> which you have made known
> for the salvation of all.

The Great Canon of St Andrew of Crete is regarded as the king of Canons and so matches the queen of Canons, or the Golden Canon, of St John of Damascus, sung on Easter night. It is a sustained expression of sorrow for sin, and reflects the deep sense of human sinfulness which permeates Orthodox spirituality. It is meant to be chanted in a spirit of contrition, and before each troparion worshippers make the sign of the cross, and bow three times, or, more usually now, once. Its two hundred and fifty troparia range over both Old and New Testaments, comparing Christians with the notable sinners of Scripture, and urging them to avoid their fate by repentance, and following the example of the great biblical saints instead. Throughout the Canon our dependence on God's mercy is stressed. For although we must repent, and demonstrate the sincerity of our repentance by the way we live, our salvation cannot be earned by our own works, but is the free gift of God's graciousness, brought into sharp focus by the willing self-offering of God in Christ on the cross.

14

Saturday of the Acathist Hymn

The Acathist hymn to the Mother of God is one of the most popular devotions in the Orthodox Church. It was written most probably in the sixth century by the famous Byzantine composer Romanus. In the fifth week of Lent it is sung at Matins on Saturday. In parish practice the service is celebrated on the previous Friday evening, and in modern Greek usage the hymn is sung not at Matins, but at Compline on Friday evening.

The Acathist hymn has twenty-four stanzas. The first twelve tell the story of the birth of Jesus, from the Annunciation to the Presentation of Christ in the temple. The second twelve form a meditation on the mystery of the incarnation, whose praise they also proclaim. To the first and subsequent odd stanzas a series of salutations to the Virgin is added, ending with the refrain "Hail, Bride without bridegroom!" The alternate stanzas end with the refrain "Alleluia!"

From Vespers

Today is made known the mystery
that existed before the foundation of the world.
The Son of God becomes the Son of Man,
so that he may share in what is worse
in order to enable me to share
in what is better.
Adam once was deceived:
he longed without success
to become God.
Now God becomes human
to make Adam god.

Let creation rejoice,
let nature exult:

in awe the archangel
approaches the Virgin,
conveys her the greeting,
our sorrow's consoling.
Glory to you, O God,
who in merciful compassion
became a human being.

From Matins

The archangel acknowledged the mystic command,
and the spirit sped to Joseph's house.
He said to the Virgin:
"He who humbled himself
and bowed the heavens and came down
dwells unchanged entire in you.
In your womb I see him
take the form of a slave,
and astonished I greet you:
Hail! Bride without bridegroom."

From the Acathist Hymn

Mother of God, our victorious leader,
we your servants offer you grateful praise,
for you have freed us from danger.
Your power is invincible:
free us from every calamity,
so that we may greet you:
Hail! Bride without bridegroom.

The chief of the angels
was sent from heaven.
Hail! he said to the Mother of God.
When he saw you, Lord, enfleshed
at the sound of his fleshless voice,
he stood still in wonder
and cried out to her:

Hail! through you joy will shine out;
Hail! through you the curse will be eclipsed;

Hail! raising of fallen Adam;
Hail! drying of Eve's tears;
Hail! height too high for human thought;
Hail! depth too deep for even angels' sight;
Hail! for you are the king's throne;
Hail! for you carry him who carries all;
Hail! star making the sun shine;
Hail! womb where God became human;
Hail! through you creation is renewed;
Hail! through you the Creator is born a child;
Hail! Bride without bridegroom.

Racked by tempestuous doubts,
Joseph the prudent was troubled.
He saw you unjoined in marriage,
and suspected you, blameless,
guilty of illicit union.
When he learnt you had conceived
by the Holy Spirit, he cried out:
Alleluia!

The shepherds heard the angels sing the praise
of the coming of Christ in the flesh.
They went quickly to the shepherd,
and saw him as an innocent lamb
who had been pastured in Mary's womb.
They sang her praises, saying:
Hail! Mother of the lamb and shepherd;
Hail! fold of spiritual sheep;
Hail! defender against invisible foes;

Hail! opener of the gates of Paradise;
Hail! for things on earth rejoice with the heavens;
Hail! perpetual voice of the apostles;
Hail! unflagging courage of the victors;
Hail! firm support for faith;
Hail! bright revelation of grace;
Hail! through you hell is stripped naked;
Hail! through you we are clothed with glory;
Hail! Bride without bridegroom.

From Matins

> Today is made known the mystery
> hidden from before the world's foundation.
> God the Word, the Word of God,
> becomes of his good pleasure
> the Virgin Mary's Son.
> And Gabriel announces the joyful good news.
> With him let us cry out:
> Hail, Mother of the Lord!

Just over a week before the beginning of Holy Week, the Saturday of the Acathist reminds us that he who suffers and dies is none other than the Word of God, the Second Person of the Trinity. He became human in Mary, who can therefore rightly be called the Mother of God, the title given her by the Third Ecumenical Council, of Ephesus, in 431.

The Orthodox Church gives special prominence to Mary, in iconography and in liturgical texts. The twenty-four stanzas of the Acathist are frequently found depicted among the fresco icons which often cover the walls and vaults of Orthodox churches. Her position in the Church derives from her role in God's plan of salvation: it was her consent which enabled God the Word to take to himself complete humanity in her womb, and to be born human as we are. Mary is never thought of apart from the incarnation. At the same time she is a figure of the Church, and the icon of her Falling Asleep, or Dormition, points us not only to her destiny, but to the destiny which awaits the whole Church, and all humankind: we are created to be united in Christ with God the Holy Trinity, and to share in the life of God in glory. That destiny is made possible for us by the passion, death and resurrection of the Christ, the Son of Mary, who is God the Son.

15

Fifth Sunday of Lent:
St Mary of Egypt

Like the commemoration on the fourth Sunday in Lent of St
John of the Ladder, that of St Mary of Egypt on the fifth is a
later addition. She has already been commemorated, as we have
seen, on the Thursday of the fifth week of Lent. The prominence
a commemoration on Sunday gives her is entirely appropriate in
Lent. For Mary is another model of repentance. A prostitute in
Alexandria, she took ship with a group of pilgrims to Jerusalem,
hoping for business during the voyage. She went up to the holy
city with the pilgrims, and out of curiosity went with them to the
Church of the Resurrection, or Holy Sepulchre, for the feast of
the Exaltation of the Holy Cross. But some invisible force barred
her entry. She realized it was her sinful way of life that stood in the
way. Confronted with the icon of the Mother of God, she re-
pented, entered the church and venerated the cross. She then
went away into the Judean desert, to live a life of great austerity.
After many years, towards the end of her life, a priest called
Zosima found her, and took her communion. Next year when he
went to look for her he found her dead.

The first canon at Matins is based on another theme, that of
the parable of the Rich Man and Lazarus (Luke 16:19-31).

From Vespers

> The stain of past sins
> prevented you from seeing holy things.
> But then your conscience,
> and perception of what you had done,
> made you, wise in God's ways,

turn to a better life.
Mother, you deserve our praise;
for when you saw the icon of God's handmaid,
you condemned your previous sins,
and so went boldly to venerate
the honored wood.

When you had worshipped joyfully
at the holy places,
you were given healing nourishment
to follow the way of virtue.
Speedily you set out
on the good journey.
You crossed the river Jordan,
and eagerly made your dwelling
where the Baptist lived.
By your way of life
you bridled your wild passions.
With courage you curbed
the disorders of our fallen nature,
mother for ever blessed.

The power of your cross, O Christ,
has worked miracles.
Even she who had been a prostitute
entered the ascetic contest.
She threw off her weakness
and bravely opposed the devil.
Now she has received the prize of victory,
she prays for us.

By the sword of abstinence
you cut off your soul's desires
and your fallen nature's passions.
By ascetic silence
you strangled sinful thoughts.
You watered the whole desert
with the streams of your tears,
and made the fruits of repentance
spring up for us.
That is why, holy mother,
we celebrate your memory.

From Matins

You have compared me,
rich in lustful desires,
to the rich man
who lived sumptuously every day.
That is why I pray:
Save me from the fire, O Savior,
as you saved Lazarus.

I have put on sensual pleasures, O Savior,
as the rich man put on fine linen
and gold jewelry and clothing.
But do not send me to the flames
as you sent him.

Make me poor like Lazarus,
I pray you, O Christ,
since by nature you are God,
and exile my sensual desires.
But make me wealthy,
like the rich man, in virtues,
so that with faith
I may proclaim your greatness.

The kingdom of God is not food and drink
but righteousness and discipline with holiness.
So the rich shall not enter it,
but those who give their wealth to the poor.
This is what the prophet David teaches:
The righteous show mercy all day long;
their delight is in the Lord,
they walk in the light
and do not stumble.
This was all written to exhort us
to fast and do good;
so that, in exchange for worldly goods,
the Lord might reward us with heavenly.

St Mary of Egypt was one of most venerated mothers of the desert, and like another Mary, of Magdala, she became in the Orthodox tradition an icon of the repentant sinner. Lent is now well advanced: there is only one week before Holy Week. Again we are reminded of the crucial importance of recognizing our sinfulness, and turning to God in sorrow for it, and with a determination to make a fresh start and live a new life. Although the insistence on ascetic discipline reflects the monastic background from which most Orthodox hymnography comes, no Christian can avoid the need to control sinful impulses and strengthen virtues.

Again, a gospel parable is given a spiritual application to us and to all Christians. Like the rich man, we are wealthy in sinful passions and lusts. Our prayer is that, repenting like Mary, we may become poor in spirit and so be saved like Lazarus, escaping the fate of the rich man.

16

Saturday of Lazarus

In St John's Gospel the raising of Lazarus is the last and greatest of the signs performed by Jesus: it proclaims him as the giver of life. It is also, paradoxically, the immediate cause of his own death, for it is what finally convinced the religious leaders of Jerusalem that they must be rid of him. So both historically and theologically it is appropriate to celebrate the raising of Lazarus as the prelude to the death and resurrection of Jesus himself. At the Liturgy today the gospel is John 11:1-45, and the theme of the raising of Lazarus dominates all services, which at the same time look forward to Christ's own resurrection.

From Vespers

We have completed the forty days
that bring us spiritual profit.
Now we ask you in your love for us:
grant us to celebrate the holy week
of your suffering and death,
so that in it we may glorify your mighty works
and your purpose for us,
too great for words.
May we sing in unison:
Glory to you, O Lord.

Lord, your voice broke the power of hell,
and your powerful word raised from the grave
him who had been dead four days.
Lazarus became the saving first-born
of a world made new.
You can do all things,
Lord, for you are king of all.
Make your servants pure
and grant them abundant mercy.

Lord, you came to Lazarus' grave
and called him by name,
to assure your disciples
of your resurrection from the dead.
Hell then was robbed:
it gave up him
who had been dead four days,
as he cried out to you:
"Lord whom we bless,
glory to you!"

Lord, you took your disciples
and came to Bethany
to wake up Lazarus.
You wept for the dead
as human beings do.
But as God you raised up
the body four days dead;
and he cried out to you, our Savior:
"O Lord whom we bless,
glory to you!"

From Compline

As a human being you wept
for Lazarus;
as God you raised him up.
You asked,
"Where have you laid him,
dead four days?"
And so, good Lord,
you gave proof of your incarnation.
By your word in the beginning,
O Word of God,
you breathed life into the clay
and joined dust to spirit.
Now by your word
you have raised up your friend
from death's corruption
and the depths of the earth.

From Matins

Before you suffered and died,
O Christ our God,
you raised Lazarus from the dead,
giving us an assurance
of the resurrection of all.
And so like the children
we too carry signs of victory
and cry out to you,
victor over death:
Hosanna in the highest!
Blessed is the one who comes
in the name of the Lord!

In the fully-developed pattern of Holy Week services in Jerusalem towards the end of the fourth century, the Saturday before Palm Sunday was dedicated to the commemoration of Lazarus, and a procession went to his tomb. The Orthodox calendar has kept this combination of days, which link the forty days of Lent with the celebration of Christ's suffering and death in Holy Week and his resurrection at Easter. Some of the hymns on the Saturday of Lazarus explicitly link this day with the triumphant entry of Christ into Jerusalem.

The texts for the Saturday of Lazarus reflect explicitly the Orthodox doctrine of the person of Christ. He is fully human, and so weeps for Lazarus. But he is also the Second Person of the Trinity, through whom all things were made, and so is able to raise Lazarus from death. We are reminded before Holy Week that the one whose suffering and death on the cross we are about to commemorate is certainly the human Jesus, but that in and through his humanity it is God who is giving himself in love to suffer and die for the salvation of the world.

The texts also present the raising of Lazarus as a prophecy of Christ's own resurrection. It therefore reassures the disciples, whose faith in Christ is to be put severely to the test by seeing the one they believed to be the Messiah suffer and die. It is too a prophecy of the resurrection of all who believe in Christ, which will be made possible by his death and resurrection.

17

Palm Sunday

The services of Palm Sunday are Vespers, celebrated on Saturday evening, Matins and the Liturgy, together of course with the Hours. Vespers on Sunday evening is the first service of Monday. But since in parish practice Matins of Monday is celebrated on Sunday evening, Vespers is relatively short, and celebrated usually earlier in the afternoon. "The Bridegroom Service," as Monday's Matins is popularly called, begins the pattern of Holy Week services, which are usually anticipated by half a day, Matins being on the evening of the day before, and Vespers in the morning.

There is no palm procession in the modern Orthodox rite, as there is in the West, but palms or other branches are blessed at Matins after the gospel reading, and then held by the people, together with candles, until the end of the service.

The theme of the services on Palm Sunday is primarily that of Jesus' entry into Jerusalem. But the raising of Lazarus also runs through them, and the coming of Christ in glory is yet another strand, while praise of his victory on the cross is present too.

From Vespers

> Today the grace of the Holy Spirit
> has brought us together.
> Taking up your cross we say:
> Blessed is he who comes
> in the name of the Lord.
> Hosanna in the highest!

> Six days before Passover
> Jesus came to Bethany,
> and his disciples came to him and said:
> "Lord, where do you want us to make the preparations

for you to eat the Passover?"
He sent them off and said:
"Go into the village opposite,
and you will find a man
carrying a jar of water.
Follow him,
and say to the owner of the house,
The Teacher says, I will keep Passover
in your house with my disciples."

Glory to you, O Christ,
seated on the throne on high,
now expected with your precious cross.
That is why the daughter of Zion is glad,
and the peoples of the world rejoice.
Children carry branches
and the disciples clothing.
The whole world has learnt to shout out to you:
"Blessed are you, Savior,
have mercy on us."

The Son and Word of the Father,
like him without beginning and eternal,
has come today to the city of Jerusalem,
sitting on a colt, a dumb animal.
The cherubim cannot look at him for fear;
yet the children honor him
with palms and branches,
and mystically sing his praises:
Hosanna in the highest
to the one who has come
to rescue all our race
which had gone astray.

Buried with you by baptism,
O Christ our God,
we have been given eternal life
by your resurrection.
We sing your praise and cry out:
Hosanna in the highest!
Blessed is the one who comes
in the name of the Lord!

From Matins

Carrying spiritual branches,
and with souls made clean,
let us joyfully cry out
with faith to Christ,
like the children,
loudly praising the Lord:
Blessed are you, Savior!
You have come into the world
to save Adam from the primal curse.
Loving humankind, you were well pleased
to become spiritually the new Adam.
Glory to you, O Word,
for you have done all things for good.

Because you have bound hell,
immortal One,
and put death to death,
and raised up the world,
the children praise you, O Christ,
with branches as victor,
and call out to you today:
"Hosanna to the Son of David!
No more," they say,
"shall babes be slain
for Mary's babe;
but you alone are crucified
for young and old, for all alike.
No more shall the sword
be drawn against us,
for your side will be pierced
by a spear."
So we rejoice and say:
Blessed is the one who comes
to call Adam back again.

Before your passion, O Christ our God,
you made plain in advance,
for our common reassurance,
the resurrection all will share.

For in Bethany, by your mighty power,
you raised Lazarus
who had been dead four days.
You gave sight to the blind,
Savior, as giver of light.
You went into the holy city
with your disciples,
sitting on the colt of a donkey,
as though borne upon the cherubim,
so fulfilling what the prophets proclaimed.
The children of the Hebrews,
with palms and branches,
came to meet you.
So do we carry branches of olive and palms,
and cry out our thanks:
Hosanna in the highest!
Blessed is the one who comes
in the name of the Lord!

From Sunday Vespers

From palms and branches,
from one divine feast to another,
let us make haste, we who believe,
to reverence Christ's passion,
that mystery of salvation.
Let us see him suffer
willingly for us.
In thanksgiving let us sing him
a song such as we should:
Lord, source of mercy
and harbor of salvation,
glory to you!

The historical background of the first hymn is the pattern of
monastic life in Palestine in the fifth and sixth centuries. Monks
would go out into the desert in ones or twos to spend Lent in
solitude. They returned to the monastery in time for the vigil on
Saturday evening before Palm Sunday, to keep Holy Week to-

gether. But Christians always gather for worship "in the Holy Spirit," and so the hymn forms an apt beginning to the Christian community's liturgical observance of those events which called it into being.

In Eastern as in Western liturgical tradition Palm Sunday is a celebration of Jesus Christ as king, as the one sent by God to establish his kingdom in the life of the world. The Orthodox hymns commemorate his entry into Jerusalem, welcomed by its people. They also speak of his present lordship at the right hand of God, and of his coming again, to establish in its fullness the reign of God which his death and resurrection have already inaugurated.

On Palm Sunday we celebrate Christ's victory over sin and death, won on the cross, and anticipated in the raising of Lazarus. In the Orthodox tradition the cross is always seen, as it is in St John's Gospel, as the symbol of victory: Christ "has reigned and triumphed from the tree," as a Western hymn says. It is sometimes said that Eastern Christianity concentrates on the resurrection, Western Christianity on the cross. That is not borne out by the texts. What is true is that the death of Jesus is presented as a victory, and that even on Good Friday the resurrection is not absent. It is also the case that the resurrection is rarely celebrated without some reference to the cross which made the new risen life possible.

18

Monday in Holy Week

On the first three days of Holy Week the pattern of services is the same. Matins in parish practice is usually anticipated the previous evening. In the morning, Vespers is celebrated, followed by Holy Communion from the sacrament reserved from the Sunday Liturgy, the two together forming the Liturgy of the Presanctified Gifts. Earlier in the morning, before Vespers, the Hours are celebrated one after the other, and at them in the course of these three days all four gospels are read, spread over the Third, Sixth and Ninth Hours.

Matins on the first three days of Holy Week is known popularly as "The Bridegroom Service." Its name comes from the troparion "Look! the bridegroom comes at midnight," and its theme is drawn from the parable of the ten bridesmaids, which forms part of the gospel read at Vespers on Tuesday evening. Three other themes run through the services on Holy Monday: the story of Joseph from Genesis, chapters 37 and 39-40; the cursing of the barren fig tree by Jesus on his way into Jerusalem, told by Matthew, 21:18-22; and the presumption of the mother of Zebedee's sons in asking for privileged places for James and John in the coming kingdom, recounted in Matthew 20:20-28. Running all through is the fourth and basic theme of the suffering of Jesus Christ.

From Matins

> Look! the bridegroom comes at midnight.
> Blessed the servant he finds watching;
> but worthless the one he finds idling.
> Take care, then, my soul:

let not sleep overcome you,
lest you be handed over to death
and shut out of the kingdom.
But be sober again and cry out:
Holy, holy, holy are you, O God:
at the prayers of the Mother of God
have mercy on us.

I who in divinity am rich
have come to serve Adam
who has become poor.
I who made him have willed
to put on his form.
I who as God cannot suffer
have come to give my life
as a ransom for him.

To lamentation let us add lamentation,
and with Jacob weep
for Joseph, wise and praised.
A slave in body,
he kept his spirit free,
and ruled all Egypt.
For God gives his servants
an imperishable crown.

Your marriage chamber, my Savior,
I see arrayed,
and I have no wedding robe,
that I might enter.
Clothe me with brightness,
giver of light,
and save me.

On the way to his voluntary passion,
the Lord said to his apostles:
"See, we are going up to Jerusalem,
and the Son of Man will be betrayed,
as it is written about him."
Let us then also go with him,
with minds made pure.
Let us be crucified with him,

and for his sake die
to the pleasures of this life,
that we may also live with him,
and hear him say:
"No longer do I ascend
to the earthly Jerusalem to suffer,
but to my Father and your Father,
to my God and your God;
and I shall raise you up
to the Jerusalem above
in the kingdom of heaven."

Lord, the mother of Zebedee's sons
failed to understand the mystery
of your hidden purpose,
and asked you to give her sons
a worldly kingdom's privilege.
But instead you promised your friends
they would drink the cup of death,
and you said you would drink this cup
before they did,
to cleanse us from our sins.
So we cry out to you:
Glory to you, our Savior.

Brothers and sisters,
let us fear the punishment of the fig tree,
withered because it bore no fruit;
and let us bring to Christ
the due fruit of repentance,
for he gives us his generous mercy.

The suffering and death of the Word of God become human for us is the background to all the services today and throughout the week. The Orthodox Church emphasizes that it is the Second Person of the Trinity, God himself, who suffers and dies in the flesh for our salvation. This leads to the use of striking paradoxes in texts about the passion, as in the second of the hymns above, based on Philippians 2:5-11. Christ suffers innocently, for he is without sin; and so in Eastern Christian tradition Joseph is seen as prefiguring him, for though innocent he was persecuted by Potiphar's wife.

The barren fig tree, cursed by Jesus because he found no figs on it, is a symbol of the judgment that will fall on us if we do not produce the fruits of repentance and holy living. Those fruits include turning our back on the pride which seeks rank and privilege for ourselves. John and James' attempt to obtain pride of place in the kingdom of God is in sharp contrast with Christ's own humility in renouncing his status as Creator in order to suffer with and for his own creatures.

The "Bridegroom" troparion used on the first three days of this week brings the theme of judgment to the fore in Orthodox Holy Week. In the Western calendar this theme has its place in the Advent season before Christmas. Its prominence here in Orthodox Holy Week reflects the early Christian belief that Christ would come during the Easter Vigil. It is entirely appropriate in the week that commemorates the passion of Jesus, since the cross of Christ is the judgment as well as the salvation of the world. Jesus, in John 12:31, says: "Now is the judgment of this world; now the ruler of this world will be driven out. And I, when I am lifted up, will draw all people to myself."

19

Tuesday in Holy Week

Matins again begins, after the usual opening psalms and litany, with the "Bridegroom" troparion, and is anticipated the previous evening. On Tuesday morning, Vespers and the rest of the Liturgy of the Presanctified Gifts is celebrated.

Two gospel parables supply the themes for today's services. One is the parable of the Wise and Foolish Bridesmaids, Matthew 25:1-13, the other is the parable of the Talents immediately following, Matthew 25:14-30. Both are included in the lengthy gospel used at Vespers, Matthew 24:36-26:2. The theme of Judas' betrayal makes its appearance, to become more prominent tomorrow and Thursday, while at Compline is introduced one of Wednesday's chief themes, the woman who anointed Jesus with fragrant ointment.

From Matins

> Let us love the bridegroom, brethren,
> and look after our lamps,
> radiant with virtues
> and right belief;
> so that, like the Lord's wise bridesmaids,
> we may go in prepared
> with him to the marriage feast.
> For the bridegroom, as God,
> gives to all the imperishable crown.
>
> Ungodly Judas, moved by greed,
> makes hostile plots against the Lord,
> and wonders how to betray him.
> He turns away from light
> and welcomes darkness.

He agrees a price
and sells him who is beyond price.
The wretched man receives his reward—
a hangman's noose and death in agony.
O Christ our God,
deliver us from a fate like his,
and grant forgiveness of sins
to those who with love
celebrate your purest passion.

I am asleep in idleness of soul,
O Christ the bridegroom,
I have no lamp burning with virtue.
Like the foolish bridesmaids
I wander off when the time comes for action.
Do not harden your heart of mercy
against me, Lord,
but drive from me dark sleep
and wake me up.
Lead me with the wise bridesmaids
into the marriage hall,
where resounds in purity
the voice of those who feast,
and never cease to sing:
"O Lord, glory to you."

Come, you who believe,
and serve the Lord eagerly,
for he gives wealth to his servants.
According to what he has entrusted to us,
let us put the talent of his grace to work.
Let one acquire wisdom through doing good,
and another celebrate the Liturgy with beauty.
Let those who have faith share the word
with those who are unaware of the mystery.
Let the wealthy be generous to the poor.
So shall we increase
what has been lent to us,
and as trustworthy stewards of his grace
we shall be counted fit
to enter the joy of our Lord.

O Christ our God,
grant us this joy,
for you love humankind.

From Compline

While you sat at supper,
O Word of God,
a woman came to you.
At your feet she wept,
and took the alabaster jar
and anointed your head with sweet oil,
you, the ointment of immortality.

"My fragrant ointment is perishable,
yours is the ointment of life,
for your name is ointment,
poured out on those worthy of it.
But set me free and forgive me,"
cried the prostitute to Christ.

Both the parables whose themes dominate the services of Holy Tuesday are understood as parables of judgment; and so they pick up and elaborate the note of judgment sounded by the "Bridegroom" troparion on each of the first three days of Holy Week. Both emphasize our own responsibility for our lives. God gives us grace: in his love he is always with us, forgiving us, strengthening us, prompting us to live in accordance with his will. But grace involves our response as well as God's initiative: we have to be willing to accept his love and forgiveness, and to accept the discipline of shaping our lives as he wants them to be. We must put the talent of his grace to work, we must ensure that the lamp of virtue is kept supplied with the oil of good works. The bridegroom, the master, will come—on Easter night. This second day of Holy Week urges us to be ready for his coming.

20

Wednesday in Holy Week

At Matins, celebrated on Tuesday evening, the troparion "Look! the bridegroom comes at midnight" is sung, as on the previous two days. But then two principal themes are interwoven in the texts: Jesus' betrayal by Judas, and his anointing by the anonymous woman in the house of Simon in Bethany—Matthew 26:6-16, the gospel read at Vespers. The hymns sung at Vespers are drawn from those of Matins, and, as on Monday and Tuesday, the service is part of the Liturgy of the Presanctified Gifts, celebrated in practice in the morning.

In the evening, Matins of Holy and Great Thursday is celebrated. In practice, the main service on Wednesday evening is often the Anointing of the Sick. This is not formally appointed here, but it attracts large numbers of people, who receive anointing not only for physical healing but also for spiritual.

From Matins

> The prostitute came up to you,
> who love humankind.
> She poured on your feet
> fragrant ointment with tears.
> By your order she was set free
> from the stench of her sins.
> Although he breathed in your grace,
> the ungracious disciple rejected it.
> He befouled himself
> and for love of money sold you.
> Glory to your compassion,
> O Christ!

> While the sinful woman brought sweet ointment,
> the disciple made a pact with sinners.

She was glad to pour out what was very costly,
he was eager to sell him who is beyond all price.
She recognized the Lord,
he cut himself off from him.
She was set free,
but Judas was enslaved to the enemy.
Terrible his indifference!
Great her repentance!
Such repentance grant also to me,
O Savior who has suffered for our sake,
and save us.

Loving Lord, I have sinned
more than the prostitute,
yet no storm of tears have I brought you.
But silently I fall in prayer at your feet,
kissing them with love;
and I implore you as Lord
to forgive me my sins,
for I cry out to you, my Savior:
Set me free from my foul deeds.

The woman who had sinned much
perceived your divinity, Lord,
and assumed the role of one who brings oil.
With mourning she brought you
before your burial fragrant ointment.
"Alas!" she said,
"all is night to me,
night dark and without moon,
night goading my passions
with the love of sin.
You bring down from the clouds
the waters of the sea:
accept my streaming tears.
You bowed down the heavens
when you emptied yourself
beyond human imagining:
hear my heart's groans.
I will kiss your pure feet
and wipe them again with my hair,

those feet whose fall at dusk
Eve heard in Paradise,
and hid herself in fear.
Who can search out my many sins
and the depths of your judgments,
Savior of my soul? Do not disregard your servant,
for your mercy is infinite."

From the Sixth Hour

Today the wicked Sanhedrin has met
and plotted in vain against you.
Today Judas, as pledge for his bargain,
receives the hangman's noose.
Caiaphas, in spite of himself,
acknowledged that one,
for the sake of all,
agreed to suffer willingly.
O Christ, our God and redeemer,
glory to you!

From Compline

The mind of the God-slayers
matched the deed of the money-greedy.
They took up weapons to kill,
he was prompted by money.
Preferring hanging to repentance,
in his sins he was deprived of life.

The woman who anointed the feet of Jesus in the house of
Simon the leper at Bethany (Mt 26:6-13) did so, Jesus said, in
preparation for his burial. St John also describes an anointing just
before Jesus' passion, performed by Mary the sister of Lazarus,
again in preparation for Jesus' burial. In St Luke's Gospel (7:36-
50) a similar incident is described, in which the woman is said to
be a sinner; and her expressions of love for Jesus are said to be her
response to her recognition that her many sins have been forgiven.
In Christian tradition the woman in all three stories came to be

identified with Mary Magdalen, who became the icon of the repentant sinner. She is therefore a model for us, as we prepare to celebrate the suffering and death of Jesus, which reconcile us to God: like her, we have sinned; like her, we repent; and like her, we want to show our love for the Savior, who has forgiven us at such cost to himself.

In the liturgical texts the woman stands in sharp contrast to Judas. The hymns for these days make much of Judas' treachery, and ascribe it to greed for money. Judas had been given every gift by Jesus, he was one of his close associates. Yet Judas showed no gratitude for all he had received; and refused, according to the texts, even to repent, although this is not true to the gospel accounts (Mt 27:3). Judas is then the warning type of the impenitent sinner, whose example should move us to follow that of the woman; for there is something of him in each one of us.

21

Holy Thursday

The services of Holy and Great Thursday commemorate the Last Supper, when Jesus anticipated his self-offering on the cross and commanded the disciples to celebrate the eucharistic meal in his remembrance. The washing of the disciples' feet is no less prominent, as the model for Christian love and service. But it was from the supper that Judas went to betray Jesus, and so set off the immediate train of events that culminated in the crucifixion. All these themes run through today's services, which begin with Matins, celebrated in parish practice on Wednesday evening. Vespers is usually anticipated on Thursday morning, and leads into the Liturgy of St Basil the Great. This combination shows that originally both were celebrated in the evening. The washing of feet forms part of the day's observances only in a relatively small number of cathedral churches and monasteries: it is not part of normal parish worship, as it has become in many Western parish churches.

From Matins

At the supper the glorious disciples
were enlightened when you washed their feet.
But upon the ungodly Judas
fell the shadow of greed,
and he handed you over,
you, the just judge,
to lawless judges.
You who love money,
see how because of money
he hanged himself.
Shun the greed which made him dare
to treat the Teacher so.

Lord, you are good to everyone:
glory to you!

Drawing near with fear
to the mystical table,
let us receive the bread
in purity of soul,
and stay with the Lord,
to see how he washes the disciples' feet
and wipes them with a towel.
Let us do as we have seen him do,
and be subject to one another,
washing each other's feet.
For so Christ himself
commanded his disciples;
but Judas, slippery slave,
took no notice.

Your marriage chamber, my Savior,
I see arrayed,
and I have no wedding robe,
that I might enter it.
Clothe me with brightness,
giver of light,
and save me.

He whom Isaiah proclaimed lamb
goes to the slaughter
of his own free will.
He gives his back to flogging
and his cheeks to striking.
He does not turn his face away
from the shame of their spitting.
He is condemned to a shameful death.
All this he accepts willingly,
though he is without sin,
so that to all he may give
resurrection from the dead.

Instructing your disciples in the mystery,
you taught them, Lord, and said:
"Friends, see that no fear parts you from me;

for if I suffer, it is for the world.
Do not stumble because of me;
for I have not come to be served,
but to serve,
and to give my life a ransom for the world.
If you are my friends,
do as I do.
Whoever wishes to be first,
must be last;
the master must be servant.
Abide in me,
that you may bear fruit;
for I am the vine of life."

From Vespers

Judas is indeed of the brood of vipers,
who ate manna in the desert,
and complained about him who fed them.
While the food was still in their mouths,
they spoke ungratefully against God.
So this ungodly man,
holding still in his mouth the bread of heaven
betrayed the Savior.
Mind filled with greed!
Inhuman daring!
He sold him who fed him,
he handed over to death
the Master he kissed.
He is indeed their lawless son,
and with them he is lost.
But, Lord, preserve us from such inhumanity,
for there is none so forebearing as you.

At your mystical supper
accept me today, Son of God,
as a communicant.
For I will not tell of the mystery
to your enemies,
nor will I give you a kiss like Judas.

> But like the thief I acknowledge you:
> Remember me, Lord,
> when you come into your kingdom.

This last troparion is sung in three places at the Liturgy: at the Great Entrance, as the communion chant, and as a postcommunion hymn. It brings together the Last Supper, the Eucharist, the betrayal, and the crucifixion, together with the vision of the kingdom of God to which the death and resurrection of Jesus open the way. So it is a particularly appropriate text for Holy Thursday. The celebration of the Liturgy today is primarily a commemoration of the Last Supper; but it is today as always a celebration of Christ's death and resurrection. It is also an anticipation of the heavenly banquet, that frequent gospel image of the kingdom of God. All the events of the next three days are anticipated in this sacramental celebration, just as the Last Supper itself was the occasion when Jesus both anticipated and accepted his own death. By sharing in Holy Communion the Christian enters into the salvation Christ has brought about by his voluntary passion, whose fruits he makes available to us in the Eucharist.

But the recurring theme of the washing of feet is a reminder to us that, if we would enter into that salvation, we must have in us "the same mind that was in Christ Jesus, who emptied himself, taking the form of a slave...and humbled himself and became obedient to the point of death—even death on a cross" (Phil 2:5ff). We shall be raised with Christ into the life of the kingdom only if we are willing to die with him to all that is sinful in ourselves and in our way of living.

22
Holy Friday

The celebration of the death of Christ begins on Thursday evening with Matins. It is known as the service of the twelve gospels because into the framework of Matins are inserted readings from all the gospels relating to the suffering, death and burial of Jesus. Each reading is followed either by antiphons, reflecting on the passion of Christ, or by parts of Matins. In the morning are celebrated the so-called "Royal Hours," the First, Third, Sixth and Ninth Hours, expanded by an Old Testament reading, epistle and gospel. Vespers is celebrated early in the afternoon. At its end the *Epitaphion,* a representation of the deposition of Christ, which has been on the altar, is brought out of the sanctuary in solemn procession by the clergy and placed on a table in the center of the church. The book of the gospels is placed upon it, and flowers are often put on it. After the dismissal the *Epitaphion* is venerated by the clergy and people, the equivalent of the veneration of the cross in the Western rite.

From Matins

What caused you, Judas, to betray the Savior?
Did he expel you from the apostles' band?
Did he deprive you of the grace of healing?
When you were at supper with the others,
did he drive you from the table?
Did he neglect you,
when he washed the others' feet?
How many good things you have forgotten!
Your ingratitude is clear to see;
but his infinite patience is plain to all,
and his great mercy.

Today the pure Virgin saw you,
Word of God, hanging on the cross.
Moved by a mother's love she cried,

and her heart was wounded grievously.
In deep anguish of spirit she groaned,
she struck her face and tore her hair.
She beat her breast and wailed:
"Ah me, divine child!
Ah me, Light of the world!
Why do you pass from my sight,
O Lamb of God?"
Then the angelic hosts trembled and said:
"O Lord beyond comprehension,
glory to you!"

You have redeemed us
from the curse of the law
by your precious blood.
Nailed to the cross,
pierced by the spear,
you became for us
the source of immortality.
Glory to you, our Savior.

From Vespers

All creation was transformed by fear
when it saw you, O Christ,
hanging on the cross.
The sun grew dark
and the foundations of the earth shook.
All things suffered
with you who created all.
For our sake you willed to suffer this:
O Lord, glory to you!

A mystery fearful and wonderful
we see happening today.
He who cannot be touched is seized;
he is tied who frees Adam from sin.
He who tries human hearts and secret thoughts
is unjustly brought to trial.
He is locked up in prison,
who shut up the abyss.
He stands before Pilate,

before whom stand and quake the powers of heaven.
By the hand of his creature
is struck the Creator.
To the cross is sentenced
the judge of alive and dead.
Hell's destroyer is buried in a grave.
Glory to you, most patient Lord:
all this you suffer in your love,
you have saved all from the curse.

With the help of Nicodemus
Joseph took you down from the tree,
you who wrap yourself in light
as in a garment.
He saw you dead, stripped, and unburied,
and in his grief and compassion
he bewailed you:
"Ah me, most sweet Jesus!
When the sun just now saw you
hanging on the cross
it wrapped itself in darkness.
The earth shook with fear
and the curtain of the temple
was torn in two.
Now I see you for my sake
submit willingly to death.
How can I bury you, my God?
How can I wrap you in a shroud?
With what hands can I touch your pure body?
What song can I sing at your passing,
O merciful Savior?
I extol your sufferings,
I praise too your burial
and your resurrection:
O Lord, glory to you!"

Noble Joseph took your pure body
down from the tree,
and wrapped it with sweet spices
in a clean linen cloth,
and laid it in a new tomb.

> To the women bringing spices,
> standing by the tomb
> the angel called out:
> "Sweet spices are for the dead,
> but Christ has shown
> that decay is foreign to him."

The texts emphasize the suffering and death of Christ as those of the Creator, crucified by his creatures. The mystery of the God who suffers and dies is at the heart of the Christian faith. The belief that in Jesus it is God himself who willingly identifies himself with the human race in its fallen state and consequent suffering is the only answer Christianity has to the question asked by Job and countless other innocent sufferers: how can this be, if there is a loving God who creates us and all the universe? There is no satisfactory intellectual answer. But Christian faith asserts that God is not remote from nor immune to the suffering of his creation. He cannot be, because he is love; and so he suffers in and with those who suffer innocently. The passion and death of Jesus is the measure of God's own involvement in human pain.

It is at the same time the measure of human sinfulness, and of God's forgiveness. The texts of the Holy Friday services include denunciations of the Jews their part in the death of Christ. The Western churches in recent years have generally tried to remove such accusations from their liturgical texts. Taken literally most Christians now find them an embarrassment. But though they remain in the Orthodox texts, we should understand these texts, like the New Testament passages which lie behind them, as referring to the whole of humanity. It is all human sin which nails Christ to the cross. Yet in Christ is embodied the love of God which cannot allow him to abandon the men and women created in his image, and which suffers until humankind comes to its senses, turns back to God, and wills to live in obedience to his commandments. "God was in Christ reconciling the world to himself." That saying of St Paul in 2 Corinthians 5:19 provides the underlying theme that runs through the Holy Friday services of the Orthodox Church.

23

Holy Saturday

Christ's burial and his descent into hell are the themes of today's services. Matins is celebrated usually on Friday evening, and includes the singing of Psalm 118 (119), with short troparia sung between its verses. Called "The Praises," these brief hymns form a prolonged meditation on the suffering and death of Jesus. Towards the end of the service the *Epitaphion* is carried in procession round the outside of the church, while the Trisagion is sung as a funeral chant. The procession over, the *Epitaphion* is returned to its place in the middle of the church. The gospel reading tells us that Christ is buried, the tomb is sealed. Christ our Passover has been sacrificed for us. But the reading of Ezekiel's prophecy of the valley of dry bones speaks already of his resurrection. The people come to kiss the *Epitaphion,* the image of the dead Christ, as they would kiss a dead person in their coffin at the end of a funeral service.

Vespers, leading into the Liturgy, is celebrated on Saturday morning, and is in fact the original Easter Vigil, whose celebration was gradually advanced, until it came to be held in the morning. Vespers includes fifteen Old Testament readings, on the themes of Passover, resurrection, and baptism. The baptismal character of the service changes into the celebration of Christ's resurrection with the singing of verses from Psalm 81 (82) before the gospel reading of the Liturgy.

From Matins

> When you, life immortal,
> went down to death,
> you slew hell
> by your bright divine light.
> When you raised the dead

109

from beneath the earth,
the heavenly powers shouted:
"Christ our God,
giver of life, glory to you!"

He who holds all things together
was lifted up on the cross,
and all creation lamented
when it saw him hang naked on the tree.
The sun hid its rays,
the stars withheld their light;
the earth shook in great fear,
the sea fled and the rocks were split.
Many tombs also were opened,
and the bodies of holy people were raised.
Hell below groaned,
and the Jews wondered how to spread
a false report about Christ's resurrection.
But the women cried out:
"This is the sabbath greatly blessed on which Christ sleeps.
But on the third day
he will rise again."

Today a grave holds him
who holds creation in the palm of his hand.
A stone covers him
who covers with glory the heavens.
Life is asleep and hell trembles,
and Adam is freed from his chains.
Glory to your saving work,
by which you have done all things!
You have given us eternal rest,
your holy resurrection from the dead.

Come, let us bless Joseph
who will be ever remembered.
He came to Pilate by night,
and asked for the Life of all:
"Give me this stranger,
who has nowhere to lay his head.
Give me this stranger,
whom his wicked disciple handed over to die.

Give me this stranger,
whom his Mother saw hanging on the cross.
With a mother's sorrow she wept and cried:
'Woe is me, my child!
Woe is me, light of my eye
and fruit of my womb whom I love!
What Simeon foretold in the temple
has happened today:
a sword pierces my soul.
But change my sadness into joy
by your resurrection.'"

From Vespers

Come, all peoples,
sing praise to Christ
and worship him:
glorify his resurrection from the dead.
For he is our God,
who has freed the universe
from the enemy's deceit.

By your passion, O Christ,
we have been freed from passions;
and by your resurrection
we have been ransomed from decay.
Glory to you, Lord!

Today hell groans and cries out:
My power has been destroyed.
I received a mortal man
as one of the dead.
But I am completely unable to keep him prisoner,
and with him I shall lose all my subjects.
I held in my power
the dead of all the ages.
But look, he is raising them all.
Glory to your cross, Lord,
and to your resurrection!

Mystically great Moses
foretold this day when he said,

> "God blessed the seventh day."
> For today is the blessed sabbath,
> today is the day of rest,
> on which the only Son of God
> rested from all his works.
> According to the divine plan
> he suffered death
> and rested in the flesh.
> He has come back
> to what he was,
> and by his resurrection
> he has given us eternal life,
> he who alone is good
> and loves humankind.

The death and burial of Christ, the eternal and immortal Word of God, constitute the greatest paradox of the Christian faith. God who cannot die lies dead in the grave; as he once rested on the seventh day from the work of creation, so today he rests in the tomb from his work of renewing creation. At one with humanity even in death, he goes down to the place of the dead, where death holds captive the fallen human race. This paradox runs through the texts for this day. But, as St John saw so clearly, Christ's death at the hands of fallen humanity is his victory over sin and death: the moment of death is the moment of glory. So his descent into hell is the harrowing of hell, the destruction of the power of death, and the restoration to life of fallen humankind.

For in Christ God himself, the Second Person of the Trinity, has taken to himself our human nature, fallen because of disobedience to God, and through his complete obedience, made perfect on the cross, has raised it up to that full communion with God for which we were created. The gates of death and hell are broken, the gates of Paradise are opened again, and the second Adam enters humankind's true home. The long pilgrimage on which the Church set out at the beginning of Lent has been accomplished. It remains only to celebrate on Easter Day all that the death of Jesus has already achieved.

24

Easter Day

The celebration of Christ's resurrection begins normally at midnight. A procession encircles the church, representing the women making their way to the tomb with spices to give proper burial to Jesus' body. In it are carried the book of the Gospels and the icon of the resurrection. Everyone carries a lighted candle. Outside the closed main door of the church it stops, and the resurrection is proclaimed. Then all enter the church, which is ablaze with light, for Matins of Easter Day, originally celebrated early on Sunday morning. It consists almost entirely of the Easter Canon, composed by St John of Damascus in the first half of the eighth century. It is a joyful proclamation, using rich and varied biblical imagery, of Christ's resurrection, of his victory over death, and of the salvation which we are all invited to enjoy. Then the Easter kiss is exchanged by everyone; and Matins ends with the Easter Homily traditionally ascribed to St John Chrysostom, Archbishop of Constantinople at the beginning of the fifth century. The Liturgy then begins, at which the gospel, the beginning of St John—associated in the West with Christmas—is traditionally chanted in as many languages as possible.

During the Procession

> Your resurrection, O Christ our Savior,
> the angels praise with song in heaven.
> Grant that we too here on earth
> may glorify you with a pure heart.

Easter Troparion

> Christ has risen from the dead,
> by death defeating death,

and those buried in the grave
he has brought back to life.

From the Easter Canon

First Ode

Day of resurrection!
Be aglow, all peoples.
The Lord's Passover!
From death to life,
from earth to heaven,
Christ our God
has brought us,
singing triumphantly.

Our senses purified,
we shall see Christ
radiant with light,
the unapproachable light,
of the resurrection.
His clarion greeting
we shall hear,
singing victoriously!

Heavens, as you should,
rejoice!
Earth, exult!
All creation,
seen and unseen,
celebrate!
For Christ has risen,
our eternal joy!

Eighth Ode

This is the chosen and holy day,
the first of all sabbaths,
the queen and lady
and feast of feasts,
triumph of triumphs,
in which we bless Christ for ever.

114

Come, let us share
in the new fruit of the vine,
in the divine gladness,
in the kingdom of Christ,
on this glorious day
of the resurrection,
praising him
as God for ever.

Lift up your eyes, Zion, look about you;
see, they come to you,
your children,
like God-kindled stars,
from west and north,
from sea and east,
praising in you
Christ for ever.

Almighty Father and Word and Spirit,
one nature united
in three hypostases,
above all being,
God most high,
into you have we been baptized,
and you we praise
throughout all ages.

We have seen the resurrection of Christ:
worship we the Lord Jesus, the holy one,
alone without sin.
We adore your cross, O Christ,
we praise and glorify your resurrection.
For you are our God,
you alone we acknowledge,
your name only we invoke.

Come, all who believe in him,
adore Christ's holy resurrection.
For, see, through the cross
joy has come to the whole world.
Always blessing the Lord,
we praise his resurrection.

For he suffered crucifixion,
and by death has killed death.

You fell asleep in mortal flesh,
O Lord and King;
but on the third day
you rose again.
You raised Adam from decay,
you did away with death:
you, the immortal Passover,
the world's salvation!

The Easter Homily of St John Chrysostom

Those who truly love God, let them take part gladly in this splendid and glorious festival.

Those who are faithful servants, let them joyfully enter into the joy of their master.

Those who are tired with fasting, let them now enjoy their reward.

Those who have worked from six in the morning, let them receive today what is owed them. Those who came after nine o'clock, let them celebrate the festival gratefully. Those who came after twelve o'clock, let them be confident, they will not be deprived. Those who waited until three in the afternoon, let them come forward without hesitation. Those who came only at five o'clock, let them not be afraid of coming so late. For the master is generous, and takes on the last as he took on the first. He gives rest to those who came at five in the afternoon, as well as to those who came at six in the morning. He rewards work done, and approves those who intended to work.

So enter, all of you, into the joy of our Lord. First and last, receive your reward together. Rich and poor, dance together. Those of you who have fasted, and those who have not fasted, rejoice today. The table is fully spread, let all enjoy it. The calf is fatted, let no one go away hungry.

No one need complain of poverty, for the universal kingdom has appeared. No one need weep for their sins, for forgiveness has risen from the grave. No one need fear death, for the Savior's death has freed us.

He has destroyed death by suffering death.
He has pillaged hell by descending into hell.
Hell was embittered when it met you, Lord, face to face below:
embittered, because it was annihilated;
embittered, because it was mocked;
embittered, because its power was destroyed;
embittered, because it was chained up.
It received a body, and encountered God. It received earth, and confronted heaven.
O death, where is your sting? O Hell, where is your victory?
Christ is risen, and you are thrown down.
Christ is risen, and the demons have fallen.
Christ is risen, and the angels rejoice.
Christ is risen, and life reigns in freedom.
Christ is risen, and no one is left dead in the grave.
For Christ has been raised from the dead, the first fruits of those who have died. To him be glory and dominion now and for ever. Amen.

Easter is the greatest festival of the Christian year in the Orthodox Church, and the Easter services abound in joyful celebration. The Resurrection Service, as Matins is often called, is attended by large crowds in Orthodox countries, even if many do not stay for the Liturgy which follows. The significance of Easter in Orthodox theology and spirituality is contained in the icon of the feast. It depicts the descent of Christ into hell after his crucifixion. Triumphant and glorious, he holds in his hand the cross, the trophy of victory, and stands on the broken gates of Hades. Beneath his feet the figure of death cowers defeated. The risen Christ takes by the hand Adam, and often Eve as well, drawing them out of their graves. Behind them David and Solomon, and other figures of the Old Testament, wait their turn to be raised to life. In form 'The Harrowing of Hell,' the icon is called simply 'The Resurrection'—a deliberately ambivalent title, for it shows both the resurrection of Jesus and that of the humanity he died to save. The Orthodox tradition preserves the emphasis of the early Christian paschal celebration: we celebrate both the

victory of Christ over sin and death on the cross, and our partici-
pation in the salvation his death and resurrection have given us;
and so at the Liturgy on Easter Day is sung this verse from St
Paul's letter to the Galatians:

> As many of you as were baptized into Christ
> have clothed yourselves with Christ.

Bibliography

The Lenten Triodion, translated from the original Greek by Mother Mary and Archimandrite Kallistos Ware (London and Boston: Faber and Faber, 1977).

Great Lent, by Alexander Schmemann (New York: St Vladimir's Seminary Press, 1974).

Egeria's Travels to the Holy Land, Newly translated with supporting documents and notes by John Wilkinson (Jerusalem: Ariel Publishing House and Warminster, England: Aris and Phillips, 1981).

Harlots of the Desert, by Benedicta Ward, SLG (London and Oxford: Mowbray, 1987). (An examination of St Mary Magdalen and St Mary of Egypt as icons of repentance.)

The Lenten Spring, by Thomas Hopko (New York: St Vladimir's Seminary Press 1983).